What readers are saying about *ThoughtWorks Anthology*

The technical depth, level of detail, and amount of new ideas/research in the essays in this book vary, but the connecting factor is that they're all very relevant in practice. The authors have managed to do something I haven't seen in quite some time—a great balance between "thought provoking" and "immediately applicable."

▶ **Stefan Tilkov**
CEO, innoQ

The anthology provides a peek into the diversity of views and perspectives held by a company that dares to take on the long-accepted tenet of the IT industry that custom software is too hard and too costly.

▶ **W. James Fischer**
Former CTO/Retired Senior Partner, Accenture

From highly successful open source projects such as CruiseControl to the ideas shared via blogs and conferences, chances are you've felt the impact of ThoughtWorks on your projects. While those of us on the outside have been left to ponder what kind of conversations took place within their walls, this book is a rare opportunity to pull back the curtain and join in the discussion—you'll be a better developer for it.

▶ **Nathaniel T. Schutta**
Author/Speaker/Teacher

Software is in many ways a team sport, and the leaders shape the software culture. Often successful organizations don't take the time to document them, and hence others don't benefit from them. This interesting collection of personal essays gives a glimpse into the culture of ThoughtWorks through some of its leaders.

▶ **Dave Thomas**
Bedarra Research Labs

The best insights in software development come from the people who solve real problems for real customers. Aside from combing through scattered blogs, though, it's nearly impossible to gain access to their insights. ThoughtWorkers have solved many real problems over the past decade, so I am truly delighted to hold a snapshot of their combined expertise in my hands.

▶ **Gregor Hohpe**
Coauthor, *Enterprise Integration Patterns*

This is an excellent collection of essays discussing the proper use of languages and tools to develop software in today's demanding industry. The authors are accomplished veterans of the software world.

▶ **Terence Parr**
ANTLR Project Lead, University of San Francisco

ThoughtWorks has done a fantastic job of pulling together a collection of essays that give the rest of us access to some of the experience and wisdom that ThoughtWorks is so well known for. This is one of those often-quoted books that shows up on every project bookshelf.

▶ **Jeff Brown**
Director North American Operations, G2One

The ThoughtWorks Anthology

Essays on Software Technology and Innovation

The ThoughtWorks Anthology
Essays on Software Technology and Innovation

Roy Singham   Martin Fowler   Rebecca J. Parsons

Neal Ford   Jeff Bay   Michael Robinson

Tiffany Lentz   Stelios Pantazopoulos

Ian Robinson   Erik Doernenburg

Julian Simpson   Dave Farley

Kristan Vingrys   James Bull

The Pragmatic Bookshelf
Raleigh, North Carolina   Dallas, Texas

Many of the designations used by manufacturers and sellers to distinguish their products are claimed as trademarks. Where those designations appear in this book, and The Pragmatic Programmers, LLC was aware of a trademark claim, the designations have been printed in initial capital letters or in all capitals. The Pragmatic Starter Kit, The Pragmatic Programmer, Pragmatic Programming, Pragmatic Bookshelf and the linking *g* device are trademarks of The Pragmatic Programmers, LLC.

Every precaution was taken in the preparation of this book. However, the publisher assumes no responsibility for errors or omissions, or for damages that may result from the use of information (including program listings) contained herein.

Our Pragmatic courses, workshops, and other products can help you and your team create better software and have more fun. For more information, as well as the latest Pragmatic titles, please visit us at

http://www.pragprog.com

ISBN-10: 1-934356-14-X

ISBN-13: 978-1-934356-14-2

Printed on acid-free paper with 50% recycled, 15% post-consumer content.

First printing, February 2008

Version: 2008-2-22

Contents

1 Introduction   **1**

2 Solving the Business Software "Last Mile"   **5**
by Roy Singham and Michael Robinson

   2.1   The Source of the "Last Mile" Problem   5
   2.2   Understanding the Problem   6
   2.3   Solving the "Last Mile" Problem   8
   2.4   People   8
   2.5   Automation   9
   2.6   Design for Automated Testing of Nonfunctional
            Requirements   10
   2.7   Decouple Design from Production Environment   12
   2.8   Versionless Software   13

3 One Lair and Twenty Ruby DSLs   **15**
by Martin Fowler

   3.1   My Lair Example   15
   3.2   Using Global Functions   18
   3.3   Using Objects   21
   3.4   Using Closures   27
   3.5   Evaluation Context   28
   3.6   Literal Collections   31
   3.7   Dynamic Reception   36
   3.8   Final Thoughts   38

4 The Lush Landscape of Languages   **39**
by Rebecca J. Parsons

   4.1   Introduction   39
   4.2   The Specimens   39
   4.3   The Variety of Varieties   43
   4.4   The Tree of Life for Languages   47
   4.5   That's All Very Interesting, But Why Should You Care?   49

5 Polyglot Programming   **51**
by Neal Ford

    5.1 Polyglot Programming 52
    5.2 Reading Files the Groovy Way 52
    5.3 JRuby and isBlank 54
    5.4 Jaskell and Functional Programming 55
    5.5 Testing Java 58
    5.6 Polyglot Programming the Future 60

6 Object Calisthenics   **61**
by Jeff Bay

    6.1 Nine Steps to Better Software Design Today 61
    6.2 The Exercise 62
    6.3 Conclusion 70

7 What Is an Iteration Manager Anyway?   **73**
by Tiffany Lentz

    7.1 What Is an Iteration Manager? 73
    7.2 What Makes a Good Iteration Manager? 74
    7.3 What an Iteration Manager Is Not 75
    7.4 The Iteration Manager and the Team 76
    7.5 The Iteration Manager and the Customer 77
    7.6 The Iteration Manager and the Iteration 78
    7.7 The Iteration Manager and the Project 79
    7.8 Conclusion 80

8 Project Vital Signs   **81**
by Stelios Pantazopoulos

    8.1 Project Vital Signs 81
    8.2 Project Vital Signs vs. Project Health 82
    8.3 Project Vital Signs vs. Information Radiator 82
    8.4 Project Vital Sign: Scope Burn-Up 83
    8.5 Project Vital Sign: Delivery Quality 86
    8.6 Project Vital Sign: Budget Burn-Down 87
    8.7 Project Vital Sign: Current State of Implementation . . 89
    8.8 Project Vital Sign: Team Perceptions 92

9   Consumer-Driven Contracts: A Service Evolution Pattern   93
by Ian Robinson

9.1   Evolving a Service: An Example   95
9.2   Schema Versioning   96
9.3   Breaking Changes   101
9.4   Consumer-Driven Contracts   103

10 Domain Annotations   113
by Erik Doernenburg

10.1   Domain-Driven Design Meets Annotations   113
10.2   Case Study: Leroy's Lorries   118
10.3   Summary   132

11 Refactoring Ant Build Files   135
by Julian Simpson

11.1   Introduction   135
11.2   Ant Refactoring Catalog   137
11.3   Summary   164
11.4   References   164
11.5   Resources   164

12 Single-Click Software Release   165
by Dave Farley

12.1   Continuous Build   165
12.2   Beyond Continuous Build   166
12.3   Full Lifecycle Continuous Integration   167
12.4   The Check-in Gate   168
12.5   The Acceptance Test Gate   170
12.6   Preparing to Deploy   170
12.7   Subsequent Test Stages   173
12.8   Automating the Process   174
12.9   Conclusion   174

13 Agile vs. Waterfall Testing for Enterprise Web Apps   177
by Kristan Vingrys

13.1   Introduction   177
13.2   Testing Life Cycle   178

13.3 Types of Testing 181

13.4 Environments 187

13.5 Issue Management 190

13.6 Tools 191

13.7 Reports and Metrics 192

13.8 Testing Roles 193

13.9 References 195

14 Pragmatic Performance Testing **197**
by James Bull

14.1 What Is Performance Testing? 197

14.2 Requirements Gathering 198

14.3 Running the Tests 203

14.4 Communication 209

14.5 Process 211

14.6 Summary 213

Bibliography **215**

Index **217**

Chapter 1

Introduction

ThoughtWorks is a collection of passionate, driven, intelligent individuals that delivers custom applications and no-nonsense consulting. Ask a ThoughtWorker what they like most about the company, and they will likely say it is the other ThoughtWorkers they get to meet, work with, and learn from. We're a mixture of geeks, managers, analysts, programmers, testers, and operations folks with varied cultural, ethnic, and educational backgrounds. This diversity of background and perspective, coupled with a passion for ideas that we share, can result in some pretty lively debates.

We have created a successful company with nearly 1,000 smart, opinionated people in six countries organized with little hierarchy and a fanatical commitment to transparency. Of course, our definition of success is not the typical one either; success must encompass client satisfaction, impact on our industry, and impact on our society. We do aim high.

The voices of many ThoughtWorkers are heard in the blogosphere, on the conference circuit, on the Web, and on the bookshelves. Indeed, part of our commitment to excellence involves ruthlessly critiquing what we've done and how we've done it to see how to improve it the next time. We're a tough bunch to satisfy. Once we've learned something, we want to tell others about it.

Our battle scars come from myriad projects in different domains, technologies, and platform choices. Although we do think (a lot) about what we do, that thinking is grounded in the real world of delivering lots of software for people. There's purity to our function that has allowed us to focus on developing software.

One doesn't generally pay a consultant to sit in meetings discussing the new HR policies, so our workdays are far more focused on delivering software than most IT professionals, resulting in a combination of pragmatism and rigor.

This anthology provides a great snapshot into the incredibly diverse set of IT problems on which ThoughtWorkers are working. This anthology strives to do more than simply present a few ways to produce better software; it grapples with the problems of realizing actual business value from the IT efforts that organizations take on. Roy's opening essay sets the tone with his call to arms for bringing about a change in the "last mile" of getting a system into the production environment. His program is broad and ambitious—nothing less than making those operational and deployment issues as core to the development process as the requirements gathering and coding itself. By remembering that success is not merely getting your code to pass your QA department and have it ready to toss over the wall at an operations team that deals with production, deployment, and the like, the team building the software knows they're not "done" until they've seen the software to the end. And Roy's advocacy goes past simply some clever redefinitions of *completion* and *success*. He calls for a rethinking of how and when stakeholders get involved. All the genius that has gone into making tools better for the coding process (for example, tools for automated builds and scripted testing, as well as refactoring) can be applied to tackling much of the "last mile" problem.

As you read through the collection, you'll see that his call gets answered repeatedly. For example, James takes on performance testing, an area that is habitually neglected and put off until the late stages of a project, when so many design decision have been baked into the code that undoing them without damaging the hard-won working business functionality for the sake of tackling performance feels like an undertaking in violation of the Second Law of Thermodynamics. James takes a suitably pragmatic approach, not simply arguing that we need the performance requirements up front (who can argue with this?) but discussing ways to get useful requirements from the stakeholders. He doesn't simply say "test early!" but actually discusses how and where these tests can be run.

Julian takes on Ant refactoring by cataloging a large number of standard refactorings and then providing clear examples for each. His essay is an excellent reference for anyone dealing with a growing and evolving build script. Dave's essay provides nice bookend symmetry to Roy's opening with his outlining of the conceptual framework around single-click deployment. He takes on some big issues, such as managing the large, unwieldy binaries that get generated and integration in the heterogeneous environments in which software is typically deployed. All the techniques that work to make business-software development effective will eventually migrate into the world of the deployment tools. Dave's essay takes that program forward.

Stelios's essay takes on communication techniques for conveying project health. He puts forth some metrics, both objective and subjective, and discusses effective ways to present them so that everyone involved has the same "dashboard" to work from every day. He's bringing the visibility of the project's vital signs to as many stakeholders as possible. This connects to another notion: a sort of project anthropology. Tiffany's essay reads like Margaret Mead reporting on her findings in Samoa. She has stumbled upon a whole new kind of project team member, the iteration manager, and tells us about how it fits into the tribe. She sees a chance to address how to organize the team a little differently to make it more effective, and hence we have a role to help work through this. Jeff's "nine rules of thumb" essay reminds me of some master talking to disciples about the Tao of programming. The rules are simple and elegant and maddeningly hard to adhere to (especially because they require any coder to "unlearn" so many habits). Rebecca's essay feels to me like she sneaks in a strong stance on the issue of "language wars" by starting out as an engaging read on classifying various languages. At first you read along, imagining Linnaeus strolling through a garden, looking at particular characteristics of the plants he sees, and then generalizing them to a framework for classifying any plant he comes along in the future. Rebecca lays down a great foundation. But her surprise comes at the end: this isn't just some survey course in some languages currently in vogue but instead a demonstration of the diversity of tools out there and that any particular "Java vs. .NET" language dispute is just the latest iteration in a never-ending conversation. But what matters is knowing what kind of problem you're trying to solve and what kind of tools you have at your disposal for tackling them. I feel like she came into a cluttered workshop, sorted the wrenches from the hammers, and put them in drawers with some labels that tell you what the items within are good for.

The remaining essays are a lot more technically focused but demonstrate more of the diversity of talent that I get to call fellow co-workers.

Ian lays out a comprehensive approach for thinking about SOA contracts that are consumer, rather than customer, driven. His essay takes another whack at the eternal problem of how to build and evolve shared services that need to adapt over time to changing business needs and do so in a way that doesn't cripple the existing consumers of that service. And Erik considers a similar problem. In a well-designed system, you decouple the domain model from infrastructure layers, but this requires that the infrastructure layer use the metadata present in the domain model. Some implicit metadata can be gleaned from what's in there such as the choice of classes to represent certain domain elements, but it doesn't really provide enough information for really rich stuff like validations. Some modern languages such as Java and C# provide for more metadata in the form annotations and attributes, and Erik explores how to exploit these features through a case study. And Martin's playful romp through various DSLs for evil megalomaniacs reminded me of when I was learning C so long ago. My reference was Kernighan and Ritchie, and I watched in amazement as they worked through a few iterations of a string copy function to bring it to a level of simplicity and elegance that seemed to elude me through all my subsequent programming efforts.

The threads of connection are everywhere in this anthology. These essays explore an ecosystem of IT problems and yet link together in all sorts of obvious and surprising ways. The breadth of topics and variety of approaches for solving them reflect the health of an environment of ideas that exists at the organization that all these authors are part of. Seeing a slice of it in the form of this collection leaves me hungry to see what else we're capable of doing.

Mike Aguilar (Vice President, ThoughtWorks)
February 15, 2008

Chapter 2

Solving the
Business Software "Last Mile"

**by Roy Singham, Founder and Chairman, and
Michael Robinson, Technology Principal**

Agile practices such as test-driven design (TDD), continuous integration (CI), pair programming, refactoring, and so on, have allowed us to deliver high-quality software quickly. Not only does the software work reliably right from the beginning, but it continues working reliably as it is modified to accommodate evolving requirements.

However, many challenges remain, particularly in the "last mile" of software development. This "last mile" is the part of the process that happens after the software satisfies the functional requirements but before the software goes into production and starts to deliver value to the business.

For software developers, particularly software developers under delivery pressure, the "last mile" is easy to overlook. However, this is increasingly the biggest stress point for business software delivery.

2.1 The Source of the "Last Mile" Problem

The "last mile" problems tends to be a situation you grow into. You may start from scratch as a small start-up with an innovative business model idea. With no existing systems, transaction data, customers, or revenue, you need a simple system to prove the viability of the business model.If it is successful, you will make further investments in features and scalability. For now, you have limited funding and therefore need to deliver the system and get results as quickly as possible.

This scenario is close to ideal for rapid deployment to production. There is no "last mile" problem. In this case, the software can go into production almost as soon as the business requirements are satisfied.

Time goes on, and your start-up has become successful and profitable. You now have many customers and two years of transaction data. You've purchased a customer relationship management (CRM) system and an accounting package, both of which have been integrated with the core business system.

The original core business system has received several new features, but now there is a new business opportunity that will require the development of a second core business system that will need to integrate with the existing systems.

At this point, your life is somewhat more complicated. Before the second core business system can be put into production, it will need to be tested for reliable operation with legacy systems and data.

Again, time passes, and your company has grown into a large, diversified, multinational, publicly traded corporation with many business lines and markets. The company has tens of thousands of employees and millions of customers. Revenues are large and growing but closely scrutinized by investors and market analysts. The original core business system now contains eight years of historical transaction data and integrates with twelve other business-critical systems. The system has been patched and extended over the years but is no longer able to keep up with the rate of transaction growth and changing business requirements. The company wants to replace the old system with a new system built from scratch to take advantage of more modern technology.

This is software with a "last mile" problem.

2.2 Understanding the Problem

Businesses fund new software development for the business value it can deliver, but new software often also represents a significant financial hazard if any of the following happens:

- The new software is unable to accommodate the number of users or volume of transactions required by the business model.
- The new software introduces corrupt data into legacy databases.
- The new software fails unpredictably or interacts with legacy systems in a way that causes them to become unstable.

- The new software exposes sensitive information to untrusted parties.
- The new software allows malicious users to perform unauthorized actions.

The business value at risk can easily exceed the business value that the new software is expected to deliver. Consequently, the larger a company grows, the more cautious it must become about introducing new software. This, in turn, causes old systems and technologies to accumulate in the production environment, rather than be replaced. The integration challenges of the accumulated legacy systems, in turn, increase the costs and risks of introducing new software, and so on.

This vicious cycle makes it progressively more difficult and expensive for a company to adapt to changing business model requirements as it grows and ages. New companies without this technical burden may be able sprint ahead of their older rivals to a certain point, but eventually they too will succumb.

Agile software development promises the rapid accommodation of changing requirements. This promise of responsiveness is increasingly attractive to businesses now that advances in information technology, ubiquitous Internet, and globalization have greatly accelerated the pace of business model innovation.

From the perspective of the business sponsors, however, software development matters only as an end-to-end process—from the time the budget is approved to the time the software is working for the business. What happens in between is of less interest. So, for the business sponsors, an agile process is only as agile as its ability to get software into production faster.

Large, long-established businesses with complex legacy systems may well need to spend three, four, or more months on installing, testing, and stabilizing a new software release to adequately ensure that the software is safe. In such an environment, agile developers may be able to implement a new feature requested from the business in a week or two, but depending on the timing of release cycles and how feature freezes are handled, it could be half a year before the feature is available for business use.

It may be tempting to view this as an agile success story—two-week turnaround!—and view the six-month delay as someone else's problem, but this view would be mistaken.

2.3 Solving the "Last Mile" Problem

An agile software development project today often looks something like this:

1. The business sponsor identifies the need.
2. The business sponsor gets funding approval.
3. The development team identifies a list of stories.
4. The development team finishes the stories.
5. The business sponsor accepts the finished stories.
6. The development team hands over the finished code.

A successful project is one where steps 3, 4, and 5 go smoothly and efficiently and the team gets to step 6 on or ahead of schedule. The end result is a piece of software that passes all acceptance tests. This piece of software is then, in effect, thrown over a wall, and if all goes well, some months later the business sponsor can start to use it.

If things do not go well, the software may be thrown back over the wall. Good developers will try to prevent this from happening with good test design, pair programming, and so on, and they may in many cases succeed. However, in projects that follow this pattern, the "last mile" process still significantly delays the delivery of business value, even when the code thrown over the wall is flawless and delivered ahead of schedule.

The "last mile" problem won't be solved until the agile software development process becomes an end-to-end software delivery process, where deployment to production issues are addressed at each and every step. We can start by reexamining the role of people and automation.

2.4 People

One of the biggest contributions of the agile software movement is the recognition that software development is fundamentally a social activity. Improve the conversation, and you improve the software. Much of the effort in adopting agile development practices has gone into breaking down the old structures of social organization and replacing them with more effective patterns and practices.

However, the focus to date has been almost entirely on the conversation between the software developers and the software users. This conversation produces good requirements and a common understanding of business objectives, but what about the nonfunctional requirements? Who owns those requirements, and how and when do they participate in the conversation? These questions often go unanswered.

The easiest way to eliminate "code over the wall" software development is simply to involve the stakeholders responsible for nonfunctional and cross-cutting requirements in the social activity of software development. Have them participate in the conversation early and often. Again, this will likely require breaking down old structures of social organization and replacing them with more effective patterns and practices.

Operations staffers, for example, need to install and configure the software once it is written. They need to monitor the system in production to ensure proper operation. They need documented procedures to restore proper operation if something goes wrong. They need to plan for the physical infrastructure requirements—memory, disks, network, power, cooling, and so on—of the system when it is initially installed and as it grows.

Support or help-desk staffers need useful error reporting from the system and effective diagnostic procedures. They need to know how to resolve simple system problems for users, and they need to know when and how to escalate serious system problems.

In many industries, regulatory compliance staffers need to ensure, for example, that systems implement legally mandated privacy protections or data retention policies. They need to ensure the system complies with mandatory auditing requirements.

Such stakeholders have real, legitimate business requirements that must be satisfied. The earlier these requirements are addressed in the development process, the sooner the software will be able to go into production. The sooner the stakeholders are brought into the conversation, the sooner and more efficiently their requirements can be addressed.

2.5 Automation

Currently, much of the "last mile" release process is manual, inefficient, and error prone and hence is time-consuming and expensive. To significantly reduce the time spent in the "last mile," we need to aggressively automate everything that can be automated. This involves changes in how software is built.

Soon after teams start to automate development processes, they quickly discover that automation has many of the same problems as software development. Build scripts need to be tested and debugged. Tests break and need to be updated. However, because these automation artifacts are often perceived as "not software," it is not unusual for teams to overlook all the hard-won wisdom about how to manage exactly these problems.

Build scripts, test scripts, installation scripts, and configuration files are all part of the end-to-end code that contributes to the final production system, and they should be treated that way. There should be no separate or unequal treatment of "development stuff" and "production stuff." Both should be maintained in the project version control repository. Both should be organized for clarity and maintained for consistency. And both should be refactored to simplify structure and reuse common functionality. Finally, every system component—operating system, application server, database, firewalls, storage systems, and so on—should support efficient automated testing. The overall system architecture should be designed for and defined in terms of automated tests.

For environments with many integrated legacy systems, it may not be practical to fully support the automated testing of integration points. In such cases, mocks of the legacy integration points are better than nothing. However, all new systems should provide test automation facilities for exposed integration points (for example, test setup, test teardown, test result logging, and retrieval).

A useful technique to validate new software prior to release to production is to "play back" live transactions from the current system for a specific time period and compare the results between systems. New systems should include facilities to support efficient automated playback testing.

2.6 Design for Automated Testing of Nonfunctional Requirements

Nonfunctional requirements (NFRs) may not be part of the system's functional specification, but they are nevertheless requirements with legitimate and often critical business value. Much of the time spent in "last mile" testing is to confirm the satisfaction of such nonfunctional requirements as system response time, system transaction throughput, system availability, system security, and so on. However, all too often, the NFR testing starts only after the software is "finished."

The right time to start NFR testing is before coding starts. Requirements for performance and resource utilization in particular need to be identified and analyzed up front, and a model needs to be created to map functional code to these requirements as development proceeds.

A typical approach to performance testing is to specify at the start of the project, for example, that "system response time for this operation should be less than five seconds." Then developers write the software. When they're done, operations staffers install the software on a preproduction system. The testers then perform the operation, look at a clock, and see how long the system takes to respond.

This approach has two major problems. First, if the operation in question is discovered to take five minutes rather than five seconds, the relevant software may well need to be completely rewritten just when people are expecting it to go into production. Second, if the development team attempts to avoid this problem by writing an automated performance test and incorporating this into the continuous integration test suite, the test results will be meaningful only to the extent the wall-clock performance of the test environment matches the wall-clock performance of the production environment. In many cases, this is not practical or affordable.

It is, however, possible to say something like "The production system can service 500 random disk accesses per second, and therefore the system cannot exceed 2,500 random disk accesses to perform this operation." Most operating system environments provide detailed performance counters that can be easily incorporated into automatic testing. The advantage of a counter-based performance testing strategy over wall-clock testing is that the tests become independent of the testing environment. If the tests can be run in more places, they can be run more often. Also, counter-based tests can be written at a much more relevant level of granularity. Consequently, the development team is more likely to learn of performance or resource problems as the software is written, which is when such problems are the cheapest and easiest to fix.

The performance and resource utilization model is part of the end-to-end delivery. It needs to be versioned, maintained, and calibrated across different environments. Library facilities to collect and expose appropriate counter data need to be provided to developers so they can easily and effectively integrate their code with the automated performance tests. If the model and tests are done well, final preproduction testing should be quick and free from unpleasant surprises.

2.7 Decouple Design from Production Environment

Continuous integration and test-driven design have been invaluable tools for producing high-quality software quickly. Rapid feedback allows the development team to eliminate errors quickly and cheaply as they arise and to work with confidence that the system functions as expected at any given point in time.

Unfortunately, the deployment to production process has so far reaped few benefits from CI and TDD. Ideally, user and operational tests of the fully integrated production environment would be easy to write, and the CI system would be able to run a comprehensive suite of such tests quickly enough to validate software as it is written. Typically, though, a number of obstacles prevent this from happening in practice.

First, production environments are often large, complex, expensive, and hard to set up. Second, end-to-end tests of such environments are often difficult to design, write, and verify. Third, even if an appropriate environment is set up and tests are written, such tests will typically run very slowly. A comprehensive suite of such tests may take days to complete.

The simple solution to the last problem is to run tests in parallel. If you can run ten tests at a time, you can run the test suite ten times as often. Unfortunately, the first problem—large, complex, expensive— makes this solution somewhat impractical. Providing and maintaining ten production environments for a development team to run tests is an unimaginable luxury in almost all cases.

If, however, the costs could be reduced, if production environments could be set up instantly, and if the costs could be shared among a number of development teams, then running large test suites in parallel becomes a much more realistic option. As it happens, recent advances in virtualization technology allow just that. Products are now available that can quickly save and restore complete virtual production environments on large arrays of cheap, commodity hardware.

Of course, if the system under development behaves differently in a virtual test environment vs. the real production environment, then this approach is fatally flawed. There will be no confidence in the automated test results and, consequently, little improvement in development or testing efficiency.

Every piece of business software has dependencies on and makes assumptions about the context of its deployment environment. These assumptions and dependencies can be either explicit or implicit. When a system has a large number of implicit assumptions and dependencies on its deployment context, it becomes challenging to write meaningful end-to-end system tests for alternative environments.

Consequently, to be able to take advantage of such environments for rapid, comprehensive system testing, system designers must identify the implicit assumptions and dependencies and make them explicit and testable, and they must systematically reduce the overall number of such assumptions and dependencies.

Once it becomes a realistic option to run a comprehensive automated system test suite, the investment required to write such a suite then becomes much more attractive. The ultimate objective is for the CI system to give the development team and operations staff confidence that the software is ready for deployment to production at any given point in time.

2.8 Versionless Software

The value of an agile process comes from reducing the end-to-end time and expense between the point a business need arises and the point when software goes into production to address that need. Taking this objective to the extreme, you can envision a situation where an individual feature is requested and goes directly into production as soon as it is finished.

This situation already exists today for certain types of small, simple web applications. Adding a new feature into production can sometimes be done in less than an hour. In this case, the developers don't need to release versions of software into production; they are able to release software feature by feature.

For large, complex, sensitive legacy environments, though, versionless software remains at best a distant aspirational goal. The release overhead of the "last mile" process requires that functionality be bundled into large, infrequent versions, and this is likely to be the case for the foreseeable future.

However, the costs of the current practice are unsustainable. The direct costs to business in wasted labor and the indirect costs of missed opportunities are enormous, and they represent a large and growing proportion of the total cost of software development.

Although we may not be able to achieve versionless software, we can certainly do much better. Many immediate improvements are easy and obvious. Many more improvements will no doubt be found if smart and motivated people look for them. Solving the "last mile" problem will not happen overnight. But, step by step, with the focus and active collaboration of all participants in the end-to-end software development process, it will happen.

Chapter 3

One Lair and Twenty Ruby DSLs

by Martin Fowler, Chief Scientist

Much of the reason for Ruby's recent popularity is its suitability as a base for writing internal domain-specific languages. Internal DSLs are domain-specific languages written using a valid subset of a host language. There's a resurgence about doing them in the Ruby at the moment.

Internal DSLs are an old idea particularly popular in Lisp circles. Many Lispers dismiss Ruby as having nothing new to offer in this space. One feature that does make Ruby interesting is the wide range of different techniques you can use in the language to develop an internal DSL. Lisp gives you some great mechanisms but relatively few compared to Ruby, which offers many options.

My purpose in this essay is to explore lots of these options for a single example so you have a sense of the possibilities and so you can consider which techniques work for you more than others.

3.1 My Lair Example

For the rest of this chapter I'll use a simple example to explore the alternative techniques. The example is a common, interesting abstract problem of configuration. You see this in all sorts of equipment: if you want x, you need to have a compatible y. You see this configuration problem when buying computers, installing software, and doing lots of other less nerdy pursuits.

For this particular case, imagine a company that specializes in providing complex equipment to evil megalomaniacs who want to conquer the world. Judging by the amount of films about them, it's a large market—and one made better by the fact that these lairs keeping getting blown up by glamorous secret agents.

So, my DSL will express the configuration rules for things that megalomaniacs put in lairs. This example DSL will involve two kinds of things: items and resources. Items are concrete things such as cameras and acid baths. Resources are amounts of stuff you need, like electricity.

I have two kinds of resources in my example: electricity and acid. I assume that resources have potentially lots of different properties that need to be matched. For instance, I'll need to check that all the items' power needs are supplied by power plants in the lair (evil geniuses don't like bothering with utilities). As a result, each resource will be implemented by its own class in my abstract representation.

For the sake of the problem, I assume resources fall into two categories, simple ones that have a small, fixed number of properties that can thus be rendered as arguments in the constructor (electricity) and complex ones with many optional properties that need lots of setting methods (acid). Acid actually has only two properties for this example, but just imagine there are dozens of them.

When it comes to items, I can say three things about them: they use resources, they provide resources, and they depend on another item that needs to be present in the lair.

Now for the curious, here's the implementation of this abstract representation. I'll use the same abstract representation for all the examples I'll discuss:

```
lairs/model.rb
```

```ruby
class Item
  attr_reader :id, :uses, :provisions, :dependencies
  def initialize id
    @id = id
    @uses = []
    @provisions = []
    @dependencies = []
  end
  def add_usage anItem
    @uses << anItem
  end
```

```ruby
  def add_provision anItem
    @provisions << anItem
  end
  def add_dependency anItem
    @dependencies << anItem
  end
end

class Acid
  attr_accessor :type, :grade
end

class Electricity
  def initialize power
    @power = power
  end
  attr_reader :power
end
```

I store any particular configuration in a configuration object:

`lairs/model.rb`

```ruby
class Configuration
  def initialize
    @items = {}
  end
  def add_item arg
    @items[arg.id] = arg
  end
  def [] arg
    return @items[arg]
  end
  def items
    @items.values
  end
end
```

For the purpose of this chapter, I'll define just a few items and their rules:

- An acid bath uses 12 units of electricity and grade-5 hydrochloric acid (HCl).

- A camera uses 1 unit of electricity.

- A small power plant provides 11 units of electricity and depends on a secure air vent in the lair.

I can state these rules in terms of the abstract representation like this:

`lairs/rules0.rb`

```
config = Configuration.new
config.add_item(Item.new(:secure_air_vent))

config.add_item(Item.new(:acid_bath))
config[:acid_bath].add_usage(Electricity.new(12))
acid = Acid.new
config[:acid_bath].add_usage(acid)
acid.type = :hcl
acid.grade = 5

config.add_item(Item.new(:camera))
config[:camera].add_usage(Electricity.new(1))

config.add_item(Item.new(:small_power_plant))
config[:small_power_plant].add_provision(Electricity.new(11))
config[:small_power_plant].add_dependency(config[:secure_air_vent])
```

Although this code populates the configuration, it isn't very fluent. The rest of this chapter explores different ways of writing code to express these rules in a better way.

3.2 Using Global Functions

Functions are the most basic structuring mechanism in programming. They provide the earliest way to structure software and to introduce domain names into a program.

So, my first attempt at a DSL might be to use a sequence of global function calls:

`lairs/rules8.rb`

```
item(:secure_air_vent)

item(:acid_bath)
uses(acid)
acid_type(:hcl)
acid_grade(5)
uses(electricity(12))

item(:camera)
uses(electricity(1))

item(:small_power_plant)
provides(electricity(11))
depends(:secure_air_vent)
```

The function names introduce the vocabulary of the DSL: **item** declares an item, and **uses** indicates that an item uses a resource.

The configuration rules in this DSL are all about relationships. When I say a camera uses 1 unit of electricity, I want to make a link between an item called *camera* and an electricity resource. In this first lair expression, this linkage is done through a context established by the sequence of commands. The line uses(electricity(1)) applies to the camera item because it immediately follows the declaration of *camera*. I might say that this relationship is defined implicitly by the *sequential context* of the statements.

As a human, you can infer the sequential context by how you read the DSL text. When processing the DSL, however, the computer needs a bit more help. To keep track of the context, I use special variables as I load the DSL; unsurprisingly, they're called *context variables*. One context variable keeps track of the current item:

lairs/builder8.rb

```
def item name
  $current_item = Item.new(name)
  $config.add_item $current_item
end

def uses resource
  $current_item.add_usage(resource)
end
```

Since I am using global functions, I need to use global variables for my context variables. This isn't that great, but as you'll see, there are ways to avoid this in many languages. Indeed, using global functions is hardly ideal either, but it serves as a starting point.

I can use the same trick to handle the properties of the acid:

lairs/builder8.rb

```
def acid
  $current_acid = Acid.new
end
def acid_type type
  $current_acid.type = type
end
```

Sequential context works for the links between an item and its resources but is not very good for handling the nonhierarchical links between dependent items. Here I need to make explicit relationships between items. I can do this by giving an item an *identifier* when I declare it (item(:secure_air_vent)) and using that identifier when I need to refer to it later (depends(:secure_air_vent). The fact that it is the small power plant that depends on the secure air vent is handled through sequential context.

A useful distinction here is that the resources are what Evans calls value objects [Eva03]. As a result, they aren't referred to other than by their owning item. Items themselves, however, can be referred to in any way in the DSL through the dependency relationship. As a result, items need some kind of identifier so that I can refer to them later.

The Ruby way of handling an identifier like this is to use a symbol data type: :secure_air_vent. A symbol in Ruby is a sequence of nonwhitespace characters beginning with a colon. Symbol data types aren't in many mainstream languages. You can think of them as like strings, but for the particular purpose of this kind of usage. As a result, you can't do many of the usual string operations on them, and they are also designed so all uses of them share the same instance. This makes them more efficient for lookups. However, I find the most important reason to use them is that they indicate my intent of how I treat them. I'm using :secure_air_vent as a symbol, not a string, so picking the right data type makes my intent clear.

Another way of doing this, of course, is to use variables. I tend to shy away from variables in a DSL. The problem with variables is that they are variable. The fact that I can put a different object in the same variable means I have to keep track of which object is in which variable. Variables are a useful facility, but they are awkward to keep track of. For DSLs I can usually avoid them. The difference between an identifier and a variable is that an identifier will always refer to the same object—it doesn't vary.

Identifiers are necessary for the dependency relationship, but they can also be used to handle resources as an alternative to using sequential context:

`lairs/rules7.rb`

```
item(:secure_air_vent)

item(:acid_bath)
uses(:acid_bath, acid(:acid_bath_acid))
acid_type(:acid_bath_acid, :hcl)
acid_grade(:acid_bath_acid, 5)
uses(:acid_bath, electricity(12))
```

```
item(:camera)
uses(:camera, electricity(1))

item(:small_power_plant)
provides(:small_power_plant, electricity(11))
depends(:small_power_plant, :secure_air_vent)
```

Using identifiers like this means I'm being explicit about the relationships, and it also allows me to avoid using global context variables. These are both usually good things: I do like being explicit, and I don't like global variables. However, the cost here is a much more verbose DSL. I think it's valuable to use some form of implicit mechanism in order to make the DSL more readable.

3.3 Using Objects

One of the principal problems of using functions as I did earlier is that I have to define global functions for the language. A large set of global functions can be difficult to manage. One of the advantages of using objects is that I can organize my functions by classes. By arranging my DSL code properly, I can keep the DSL functions collected together and out of any global function space.

Class Methods and Method Chaining

The most obvious way to control the scope of methods in an object-oriented language is to use class methods. Class methods do help scope the use of functions but also introduce repetition because the class name has to be used with each call. I can reduce the amount of that repetition considerably by pairing the class methods with method chaining, as in this example:

lairs/rules11.rb

```
Configuration.item(:secure_air_vent)

Configuration.item(:acid_bath).
    uses(Resources.acid.
      set_type(:hcl).
      set_grade(5)).
    uses(Resources.electricity(12))

Configuration.item(:camera).uses(Resources.electricity(1))

Configuration.item(:small_power_plant).
    provides(Resources.electricity(11)).
    depends_on(:secure_air_vent)
```

Here I begin each of my DSL clauses with a call to a class method. That class method returns an object that is used as a receiver for the next call. I can then repeatedly return the object for the next call to chain together multiple method calls. In some places, the method chaining becomes a little awkward, so I use class methods again.

It's worth digging into this example in more detail so you can see what's happening. As you do this, remember that this example does have some faults that I'll explore, and remedy, in some later examples.

I'll begin with the opening of the definition of an item:

`lairs/builder11.rb`

```ruby
def self.item arg
  new_item = Item.new(arg)
  @@current.add_item new_item
  return new_item
end
```

This method creates a new item, puts it into a configuration stored in a class variable, and returns it. Returning the newly created item is the key here, because this sets up the method chain.

`lairs/builder11.rb`

```ruby
def provides arg
  add_provision arg
  return self
end
```

The provides method just calls the regular adder but again returns itself. This continues the chain, and the other methods work the same way.

Using method chaining like this is at odds with a lot of good programming advice. In many languages the convention is that modifiers (methods that change an object's state) do not return anything. This follows the principle of command query separation, which is a good and useful principle and one that's worth following most of the time. Unfortunately, it is at odds with a flowing internal DSL. As a result, DSL writers usually decide to drop this principle while they are within DSL code in order to support method chaining. This example also uses method chaining to set the type and grade of acid.

A further change from regular code guidelines is a different approach to formatting. In this case, I've laid out the code to emphasize the hierarchy that the DSL suggests. With method chaining you often see method calls broken over newlines.

As well as demonstrating method chaining, this example demonstrates how to use a factory class to create resources. Rather than add methods to the Electricity class, I define a resources class that contains class methods to create instances of electricity and acid. Such factories are often called *class factories* or *static factories* because they contain only class (static) methods for creating appropriate objects. They can often make DSLs more readable, and you avoid putting extra methods on the actual model classes.

This highlights one of the problems with this DSL fragment. To make this work, I have to add a number of methods to the domain classes—methods that don't sit well. Most methods on an object should make sense as individual calls. But DSL methods are written to make sense within the context of DSL expressions. As a result, the naming, as well as principles such as command query separation, are different. Furthermore, DSL methods are very context specific, and they should be used only within DSL expressions when creating objects. Basically, the principles for good DSL methods aren't the same as what makes regular methods work effectively.

Expression Builder

A way of avoiding these clashes between DSLs and regular APIs is to use the Expression Builder pattern. Essentially this says that the methods that are used in a DSL should be defined on a separate object that creates the real domain object. You can use the Expression Builder pattern in a couple of ways. One route here is to use the same DSL language but to create builder objects instead of domain objects.

To do this, I can change my initial class method call to return a different item builder object:

`lairs/builder12.rb`

```
def self.item arg
  new_item = ItemBuilder.new(arg)
  @@current.add_item new_item.subject
  return new_item
end
```

The item builder supports the DSL methods and translates these onto methods on the real item object.

lairs/builder12.rb

```
attr_reader :subject
def initialize arg
  @subject = Item.new arg
end
def provides arg
  subject.add_provision arg.subject
  return self
end
```

Of course, when I start doing this, I can completely break free of the API of my domain objects and write my DSL more clearly. Consider this:

lairs/rules14.rb

```
ConfigurationBuilder.
  item(:secure_air_vent).
  item(:acid_bath).
    uses(Resources.acid.
        type(:hcl).
        grade(5)).
    uses(Resources.electricity(12)).
  item(:camera).uses(Resources.electricity(1)).
  item(:small_power_plant).
    provides(Resources.electricity(11)).
    depends_on(:secure_air_vent)
```

Here I use a builder from the beginning and use method chaining on the builder itself. Not only does this remove some repetition, but it also avoids the icky class variable. The first call is a class method that creates a new instance of configuration builder:

lairs/builder14.rb

```
def self.item arg
  builder = ConfigurationBuilder.new
  builder.item arg
end
def initialize
  @subject = Configuration.new
end
def item arg
  result = ItemBuilder.new self, arg
  @subject.add_item result.subject
  return result
end
```

I create the configuration builder and immediately call the item method on the new instance. The instance method gives me a new item builder and returns it for further processing. I have the odd case here of a class method that has the same name as an instance method. Usually

I'd avoid this because it's a recipe for confusion, but again I break my usual API rules because it makes for a smoother DSL.

The item builder has the same methods that you saw before for capturing information about the item. In addition, it needs its own item method to handle when you want to start defining a new item.

lairs/builder14.rb
```
def item arg
  @parent.item arg
end
def initialize parent, arg
  @parent = parent
  @subject = Item.new arg
end
```

This need to revert to the parent is one reason why I pass the configuration builder as a parent to the item builder when I create it. The other reason is to allow the item builder to look up other items when recording dependencies.

lairs/builder14.rb
```
def depends_on arg
  subject.add_dependency(configuration[arg])
  return self
end
def configuration
  return @parent.subject
end
```

For the previous cases, I had to look up from a global or class variable to do this.

A final refinement is that I renamed the methods on the acid builder to make them read better since the builder frees me from worrying about name clashes with the underlying domain object.

This use of Expression Builder, making a builder object for each domain object, isn't the only way to use Expression Builder. Another route is to have a single object that acts as the builder. Here's how this works with the same DSL as you just saw:

lairs/builder13.rb
```
def self.item arg
  result = self.new
  result.item arg
  return result
end
```

```ruby
def initialize
  @subject = Configuration.new
end
def item arg
  @current_item = Item.new(arg)
  @subject.add_item @current_item
  return self
end
```

Instead of creating new objects, I use context variables to keep track of the item on which I am currently working. This also means I don't have to define the parent's forwarding methods.

More Chaining

Since chaining is a good tool, can you use it all the time? Can you eliminate the resources factory? Indeed, you can. The resulting DSL code looks like this:

lairs/rules2.rb

```ruby
ConfigurationBuilder.
  item(:secure_air_vent).

  item(:acid_bath).
    uses.acid.
      type(:hcl).
      grade(5).
    uses.electricity(12).

  item(:camera).uses.electricity(1).

  item(:small_power_plant).
    provides.electricity(11).
    depends_on(:secure_air_vent)
```

(Note that I've added some blank lines to help the readability—Ruby is tolerant that way.)

The choice between using method chaining and parameters is a constant choice to make. When your parameter is a literal, such as grade(5), then using method chaining is going to be very complicated, while parameters are really easy. I tend to prefer really easy over very complicated, so that's a straightforward choice. The tricky one is between uses.electricity... and uses(Resources.electricity....

As you use method chains more, you add complexity to the builder. This is particularly the case when you start to involve subsidiary objects. This is a good example of this kind of complication. Resources are used in two contexts, either following uses or following provides. As a result, if you're using method chaining, you have to keep track of which case you're in so you can respond to the call to electricity correctly.

On the other hand, the issue with using parameters is that you have lost the scoping control that method chaining gives you, so you have to provide some scope to the parameter creation—as in this case using a class method on the factory. Quoting factory names is one of those repetitive awkwardness things that I like to avoid.

Another issue with parameters is that it may not make sense for the writer of the DSL as to when to use one or the other, which makes it harder to write DSL expressions.

My advice here is tentative, because I haven't had enough experience to guide you. Certainly use method chaining, because there is a lot of support for it as a technique. While you use it, however, pay attention to the complexity of dealing with the method chains. Once the complexity of implementing the builder begins to get messy (I realize that's a very vague indicator), introduce parameters. I'll show a few other techniques later for introducing parameters that help you avoid the repetition of class factories, but these do depend on your host language.

3.4 Using Closures

Closures are an increasingly common feature of languages, particularly dynamic languages that are popular for internal DSL work. They work very nicely for DSLs because they provide a simple way of introducing new contexts in a hierarchic structure. Here is the lairs example using closures:

`lairs/rules3.rb`
```ruby
ConfigurationBuilder.start do |config|
  config.item :secure_air_vent

  config.item(:acid_bath) do |item|
    item.uses(Resources.acid) do |acid|
      acid.type = :hcl
      acid.grade = 5
    end
    item.uses(Resources.electricity(12))
  end

  config.item(:camera) do |item|
    item.uses(Resources.electricity(1))
  end
```

```
config.item(:small_power_plant) do |item|
  item.provides(Resources.electricity(11))
  item.depends_on(:secure_air_vent)
end
end
```

A feature of this example is it uses a clear receiver for each method call and does not use method chaining. The receivers are set up using the closure syntax of the host language, which makes it easy to nest method calls in a way that fits very nicely with the hierarchic structure that you tend to have in a DSL.

An immediate visual advantage of this approach is that the natural nesting of the host language mirrors the nesting of the DSL code. This makes it easy to lay out the code easily. The variables used to hold the language elements (for example, item and acid) are properly constrained within their blocks by the host language structure.

Using explicit receivers means you don't have to use method chaining. This means you may be able to avoid using builders when the domain object's own API works. In this case, I used a builder for item but the actual domain object for acid.

One limitation for this technique is that you need to have closures in your language. Although you can use temporary variables to do something vaguely similar, this exposes you to all the problems of temps since they aren't well scoped unless you add separate scoping mechanisms. With or without extra scoping, the resulting code doesn't have the flow that I look for in a DSL, and it is very prone to errors. Closures avoid this by combining the scoping and the variable definition.

3.5 Evaluation Context

In my discussion so far, I haven't talked about the overall context in which the DSL code is being evaluated. That is, if I mention a function call or data item without a receiver, how does this mention get resolved? The assumption so far is that the context is global, so a function foo() is assumed to be a global function. I've talked about using method chains and class methods to allow you to use functions in other scopes, but I can also alter the scope of the entire DSL program text.

The most straightforward way to do this is to embed the program text into a class. This way the code can take advantage of methods and fields defined elsewhere for that class. In languages that support open classes, this can done directly in a class; otherwise, you can use a subclass.

Here's an example of this style:

`lairs/rules17.rb`

```ruby
class PrimaryConfigurationRules < ConfigurationBuilder
  def run
    item(:secure_air_vent)

    item(:acid_bath).
      uses(acid.
        type(:hcl).
        grade(5)).
      uses(electricity(12))

    item(:camera).uses(electricity(1))

    item(:small_power_plant).
      provides(electricity(11)).
      depends_on(:secure_air_vent)
  end
end
```

Placing the DSL text in a subclass allows me to do several things that aren't possible when I run the code in a global execution context. I no longer have to use method chaining for the successive calls to item, because I can make item a method of configuration builder. Similarly, I can define acid and electricity as methods of configuration builder and avoid the need for static factories.

The downside of this is that I have the addition of the class and method headers and footers to my DSL text.

In this case, I've shown evaluating the text in the context of an object instance. This is useful because it allows access to instance variables. You can also do this for a class context by using class methods. Usually I prefer an instance context, since that allows me to create a builder instance, use it for evaluation, and then discard the instance. That way I keep my evaluations isolated from each other, which avoids the risk of leftover data from one messing up another (a particularly nasty risk if concurrency is involved).

Ruby offers a particularly nice way to have and eat your cake here. Ruby has a method called instance_eval, which can take some code, either as a string or as a block, and evaluate in the context of an object instance. This allows you to have only the DSL text of this example in a file but still adjust the evaluation context. The result looks something like this:

`lairs/rules1.rb`

```
item :secure_air_vent

item(:acid_bath).
  uses(acid.
       type(:hcl).
       grade(5)).
  uses(electricity(12))

item(:camera).uses(electricity(1))

item(:small_power_plant).
  provides(electricity(11)).
  depends_on(:secure_air_vent)
```

Some languages allow you to combine closures and alter the evaluation context. So, Ruby allows you take code defined with a closure and pass it to instance_eval to be evaluated against an object instance. Using this allows me to write my DSL text like this:

`lairs/rules18.rb`

```
item :secure_air_vent

item(:acid_bath) do
  uses(acid) do
    type :hcl
    grade 5
  end
  uses(electricity(12))
end

item(:camera) do
  uses(electricity(1))
end

item(:small_power_plant) do
  provides(electricity(11))
  depends_on(:secure_air_vent)
end
```

The result is quite attractive. I have the structure of closures without having the repetition of the block arguments as explicit receivers. However, this is a technique that you need to be wary of. The switch in block context is likely to cause a lot of confusion. In each block, the pseudo-variable self refers to a different object, which can easily confuse the DSL writer. It also makes things awkward if you actually need access to the normal self within the block.

This confusion was seen in practice during the development of Ruby's builder library. Early versions used instance_eval, but practice found it confusing and difficult to use. Jim Weirich (the author of the Ruby builder library) concluded that switching evaluation context like this isn't a good idea for DSLs that are written by programmers because it violates the expectations of the host language (a concern echoed by other Rubyist DSLers). This is much less of an issue if the DSLs are targeted for nonprogrammers, since they don't have these expectations. My sense is that the more an internal DSL integrates with the host language, the less you'd want to do something like this that changes the regular expectations of the language. For mini-languages that aren't intended to look like the host language so much, like my configuration example, then the benefit of an easier-to-read language becomes greater.

3.6 Literal Collections

Function call syntax is an important structuring mechanism for internal DSLs. Indeed, for many languages it's pretty much the only mechanism available. However, another useful mechanism available in some languages is the ability to write literal collections and use them freely in expressions. This ability is limited in many languages either because you don't have a convenient syntax for literal collections or because you can't use these literals in all the places that you might like.

Two kinds of literal collections are useful: lists and maps (aka hashes, dictionaries, and associative arrays). Most modern languages provide these objects in libraries, together with a reasonable API to manipulate them. Both structures are handy for DSL writing, although any Lisper will tell you that you can simulate maps with lists.

Here is an example that uses literal data structures for the definition of acid:

`lairs/rules20.rb`

```
item :secure_air_vent

item(:acid_bath) do
  uses(acid(:type => :hcl, :grade => 5))
  uses(electricity(12))
end

item(:camera) do
  uses(electricity(1))
end
```

```
item(:small_power_plant) do
  provides(electricity(11))
  depends_on(:secure_air_vent)
end
```

For this case I am mixing function calls and literal collections and taking advantage of Ruby's ability to eliminate bracketing when there's no ambiguity. The acid function looks like this:

`lairs/builder20.rb`

```
def acid args
  result = Acid.new
  result.grade = args[:grade]
  result.type = args[:type]
  return result
end
```

Using a literal hash as an argument is a common idiom in Ruby (one of its Perlish influences). It works very well for functions such as creation methods that have lots of optional arguments. In this case, not only does it provide a clean DSL syntax, but it also means I can avoid having builders for acid and electricity—just creating the objects I need directly.

What happens if I take the use of literals further, such as replacing the function calls for uses, provides, and depends_on with a map?

`lairs/rules4.rb`

```
item :secure_air_vent

item :acid_bath,
  :uses => [acid(:type => :hcl,
                 :grade => 5) ,
            electricity(12)]

item :camera,
  :uses => electricity(1)

item :small_power_plant,
  :provides => electricity(11),
  :depends_on => :secure_air_vent
```

It's a mixed result that shows both the strength and the weakness of this approach. For the small power plant, it works very nicely because it's simple. The awkwardness lies in more complicated cases like the acid bath. Here I have two resources that the acid bath depends on; as a result, I need to put the acid and electricity calls in a list. Once I start nesting things inside literal maps, it starts getting harder to see what's happening.

This further step also complicates the implementation. The call to item involves both the name and the map. Ruby treats this as a *name* argument followed by a multiarg of name-value pairs.

`lairs/builder4.rb`

```ruby
def item name, *args
  newItem = Item.new name
  process_item_args(newItem, args) unless args.empty?
  @config.add_item newItem
  return self
end
```

The function needs to switch on the key in order to process each clause; furthermore, it needs to deal with the fact that the value may be a single element or a list.

`lairs/builder4.rb`

```ruby
def process_item_args anItem, args
  args[0].each_pair do |key, value|
    case key
    when :depends_on
      oneOrMany(value) {|i| anItem.add_dependency(@config[i])}
    when :uses
      oneOrMany(value) {|r| anItem.add_usage r}
    when :provides
      oneOrMany(value) {|i| anItem.add_provision i}
    end
  end
end
def oneOrMany(obj, &block)
  if obj.kind_of? Array
    obj.each(&block)
  else
    yield obj
  end
end
```

When you have a situation like this, where the value may be single or a list, it's often easier to use a list for the whole thing:

`lairs/rules21.rb`

```ruby
item :secure_air_vent

item :acid_bath,
  [:uses,
    acid(:type => :hcl, :grade => 5),
    electricity(12)]

item :camera,
  [:uses, electricity(1)]
```

```
item :small_power_plant,
  [:provides, electricity(11)],
  [:depends_on,  :secure_air_vent]
```

Here the arguments to the item method are the name of the item and a list (rather than a hash). The first item of the list is the key, and the remaining items in the list are the values. (This is the way Lispers treat hashes as lists.) This approach reduces the nesting and is easier to process.

lairs/builder21.rb

```ruby
def item name, *args
  newItem = Item.new name
  process_item_args(newItem, args) unless args.empty?
  @config.add_item newItem
  return self
end
def process_item_args anItem, args
  args.each do |e|
    case e.head
    when :depends_on
      e.tail.each {|i| anItem.add_dependency(@config[i])}
    when :uses
      e.tail.each {|r| anItem.add_usage r}
    when :provides
      e.tail.each {|i| anItem.add_provision i}
    end
  end
end
```

The important trick here is to think of a list as a head and tail rather than as numbered elements. So, don't replace a hash by a two-element list because this gains you nothing. Instead, treat the key as the head of the list, and flatten all the values in the tail. This way you don't have to embed one collection inside another.

Head and tail aren't in Ruby's list class (called Array) by default but are trivial to add:

lairs/builder21.rb

```ruby
class Array
  def tail
    self[1..-1]
  end
  alias head first
end
```

Before I leave the topic of using literal collections, it's worth mentioning the ultimate forms of each. Here is the whole configuration using primarily maps with lists when needed:

`lairs/rules22.rb`

```
{:items => [
  {:id => :secure_air_vent},
  {:id => :acid_bath,
    :uses => [
      [:acid, {:type => :hcl, :grade => 5}],
      [:electricity, 12]]},
  {:id => :camera,
    :uses => [:electricity, 1]},
  {:id => :small_power_plant,
    :provides => [:electricity, 11],
    :depends_on => :secure_air_vent}
]}
```

And here it is with only lists, what you might call Greenspun Form:

`lairs/rules6.rb`

```
[
  [:item, :secure_air_vent],

  [:item, :acid_bath,
    [:uses,
      [:acid,
        [:type, :hcl],
        [:grade, 5]],
      [:electricity, 12]]],

  [:item, :camera,
    [:uses, [:electricity, 1]]],

  [:item, :small_power_plant,
    [:provides, [:electricity, 11]],
    [:depends_on, :secure_air_vent]]]
```

Variable Argument Methods

Some languages define variable argument methods, which are a useful technique to use literal lists in the context of a function call. In the following version, I use them to have a single call to the uses method:

`lairs/rules24.rb`

```
item :secure_air_vent

item(:acid_bath) do
  uses(acid(:type => :hcl, :grade => 5),
       electricity(12))
end
```

```
item(:camera) do
  uses(electricity(1))
end

item(:small_power_plant) do
  provides(electricity(11))
  depends_on(:secure_air_vent)
end
```

Using a varargs method is handy in situations like this when you want
to group a list together in a method call, particularly if the language is
picky about where you can place literal lists.

3.7 Dynamic Reception

One of the benefits of dynamic programming languages is that they can
respond effectively to method calls that are not defined on the receiving
object.

We'll explore that sentence a bit more with my example. So far, I've
assumed that the resources in my lair are a relatively fixed set, fixed
enough that I am happy to write specific code to handle them. What if
this wasn't the case? What if there are many resources and I wanted to
include them in the configuration as part of the configuration?

`lairs/rules23.rb`

```
resource :electricity, :power
resource :acid, :type, :grade

item :secure_air_vent

item(:acid_bath).
  uses(acid(:type => :hcl, :grade => 5)).
  uses(electricity(:power => 12))

item(:camera).
  uses(electricity(:power => 1))

item(:small_power_plant).
  provides(electricity(:power => 11)).
  depends_on(:secure_air_vent)
```

In this case, I still want to have electricity and acid as calls on the
builder. I want it to construct the newly defined resources in those
methods, but I don't want to define the methods, since they should be
inferred from the resources.

A way to do this in Ruby is to override method_missing. In Ruby, if an object receives a call for a method that it doesn't know, then it executes its method_missing method. This method by default is inherited from the Object class and throws an exception. The trick is that you can override this method to do something more interesting.

First I prepare the ground in the calls to the resource method:

`lairs/builder23.rb`

```
def resource name, *attributes
  attributes << :name
  new_resource = Struct.new(*attributes)
  @configuration.add_resource_type name, new_resource
end
```

Ruby has a facility for creating anonymous classes called *structs*. So, when I'm asked for a resource, I define a struct for it, naming it after the first argument to the resource call and giving it a property for each subsequent argument. I also add a name argument. I store these structs on the configuration.

Next I override method_missing to see whether the method name corresponds to one of my new structs; if so, I load up the struct based on the arguments to the call—using a literal dictionary helps with this.

`lairs/builder23.rb`

```
def method_missing sym, *args
  super sym, *args unless @configuration.resource_names.include? sym
  obj = @configuration.resource_type(sym).new
  obj[:name] = sym
  args[0].each_pair do |key, value|
    obj[key] = value
  end
  return obj
end
```

As with any time I use method missing, I first look to see whether I can recognize the call. If not, I call super, which in this case would lead to an exception.

Most dynamic languages have the facility to override the handler for an unknown method. It's a powerful technique but one that needs to be used carefully. It's a mechanism that allows you to alter the method dispatch system of your program. Use it unwisely, and you can seriously confuse anyone who reads your program.

Ruby's builder library, written by Jim Weirich, is a wonderful demonstration of how you can use this. Builder's purpose is to generate XML markup, and it uses closures and method_missing to do this in a very readable way.

A simple example shows how nice it looks. This code:

`lairs/frags`

```
builder = Builder::XmlMarkup.new("", 2)
puts builder.person do |b|
  b.name("jim")
  b.phone("555-1234", "local"=>"yes")
  b.address("Cincinnati")
end
```

generates this markup:

`lairs/frags`

```
<person>
  <name>jim</name>
  <phone local="yes">555-1234</phone>
  <address>Cincinnati</address>
</person>
```

3.8 Final Thoughts

A couple of years ago Dave Thomas talked about the notion of code *katas* on his blog. The idea of a kata was a simple problem that you could solve lots of different ways to explore how different solutions worked and the trade-offs between them. This essay is such an exercise. It doesn't come to any definitive conclusions, but it does help explore the many options Ruby gives you in forming internal DSLs—and many of these options are available in other languages too.

Chapter 4

The Lush Landscape of Languages

by Rebecca J. Parsons, Chief Technology Officer

4.1 Introduction

A botanist, wandering through a field alive with plant life, marvels at the diversity and likely identifies the different species encountered there. The same is true of computer scientists marveling at the diversity of computer languages and categorizing them on the basis of their characteristics. Even with that, understanding these characteristics provides a strong basis for understanding new entries into the wonderful world of languages.

4.2 The Specimens

Whereas for plants and animals the characteristics are color, size, leaf shape, flowers, fruit, and thorns, computer-language characteristics deal with issues such as the types of statements available, the way types are handled, the way the language itself is implemented, and the basic organizing principle for programs. Given this difference in the kinds of characteristics, it shouldn't be surprising that languages can fit in many categories; plant classification is much more straightforward in that way. In this essay, we'll examine some specimens and start to develop a tree of life for languages. We'll look at old and new languages, paying particular attention to things for which particular languages are known.

Consider first an old faithful language, Fortran. Fortran in its many incarnations, long the king for hardcore scientific computation, is a classic language with some fairly simple language characteristics. Assignment statements manipulate the state of memory through the use of variable names. Other statements access that memory state and perform computations. Fortran is a classic *imperative* programming language. Imperative languages are often also referred to as *procedural* languages because the basic organization mechanism for statements is the procedure. However, these language characteristics are quite different, and thus it is useful to continue to distinguish between them.

Fortran is also a *static* language, in that programs are compiled and linked and then are ready to load and execute. The compiler translates the source program into machine language, performs optimizations, and is also responsible for declaring whether a program is syntactically legal.

Now, let's consider another classic programming language, Lisp, considered for a time to be almost synonymous with artificial intelligence, although it was more widely used than that. The acronym LISP is jokingly expanded as "Lots (of) insignificant silly parentheses" along with many other variants, but the language has several notable characteristics. Lisp is a *functional* programming language, not to be confused with procedural. The basic building blocks of Lisp programs are functions, in the mathematical sense. Pure functions manipulate data passed in as parameters and return a value; the value returned is always the same if the same input parameters are provided. Thus, pure functions have no memory or no state that can be saved from one invocation to the next.

Lisp is also a *dynamic* language. This language characteristic refers to when particular decisions or computations are made. Dynamic languages perform many of the functions that a compiler performs during execution. So, the "code, compile, test, pound desk, and repeat" cycle of program development in a static language becomes "code, test, pound desk, and repeat" in a dynamic language. The program is directly executed. The increasing popularity of virtual machines such as the CLR and the JVM are making this particular distinction less precise, but the class of dynamic languages is an important one.

Lisp is also *dynamically* typed. In dynamically typed languages, the type of a particular value is not determined until the statement is executed. Thus, there is no notion of defining a variable to be of a particular type.

A variable has the type of whatever value it currently holds. A variable X could be an integer in one instance, and then the next reference might be to a list or a boolean. Dynamic and dynamically typed languages are not the same set of languages; they cover different types of language characteristics, and their implementations are not tied to each other.

Now, let's move to a more modern language, Java. Java is an *object-oriented* (OO) programming language since the major organizational unit in a Java program is an object. Conceptually, an object is a collection of state variables and methods. Objects are members of a class that specifies what state and methods an object contains. Objects of the same class are related, but they are distinct entities. There are competing definitions for what is actually necessary and sufficient to be considered an OO language, but almost all definitions include the features of inheritance and encapsulation. *Inheritance* is a way for classes and thus objects to be related to each other. A subclass inherits all the components of its superclass and may then extend the class definition with new methods or state or override some of the existing methods. *Encapsulation* is a technique to implement information hiding. The details of the object's implementation should be hidden behind interfaces to reduce implementation dependences. *Polymorphism*, the ability for a particular function to operate on items of different types of objects, is also often considered a necessary feature for OO languages, although other languages also exhibit polymorphism. Similarly, encapsulation isn't a discriminating characteristic of OO languages either, in that this same approach can be used in many other languages.

Java, though, shares many constructs with the curly-brace languages, C and C++, and thus it also has some imperative characteristics; it is not a pure OO language.

The Ruby language is currently a darling of the IT press. Ruby is an OO language, a dynamic language, and a dynamically typed language. Ruby has a strong extension mechanism and also provides support for functional and even procedural programming.

Now let's consider Haskell, a less well-known language (although it's getting more and more recognition as time goes on). Haskell is a pure functional language in that, unlike Lisp, there are no imperative constructs. The language is *statically typed*, using *type inference* to reduce the number of explicit type declarations. Haskell also differs significantly from other languages in that the language semantics are *lazy*. A lazy language is one that never evaluates anything that isn't needed to determine the final result of the program. This laziness applies to parts of data items as well; the need for the first element of the list means that only the first element (and no others) are calculated. This difference in the execution semantics is often overlooked in the recent mentions of Haskell, but lazy semantics make Haskell programming a very different exercise than other functional languages.

Let's consider a very different example, SQL. SQL is the common query language for accessing data in a relational database. SQL is a declarative language. A program in a *declarative* language specifies what is to be computed, not how to compute it. In the case of SQL, a statement defines the characteristics of the desired data, not how to go about finding the data. Prolog is another well-known declarative language; a Prolog program consists of logical assertions—axioms and inference rules—that describe the state of the system. The execution of a Prolog program consists of answering questions about the logical provability of assertions relative to the state as defined by the axioms and inference rules. The computational model for Prolog is the algorithm that draws conclusions from the assertions, rather than an abstract computer model that describes the actual computation.

Many consider this definition of declarative languages to be unhelpful. One way to think about the definition, though, is to consider what you can determine about the computation that will occur based on looking at a particular statement. In a nondeclarative language, the statement in the language specifies what computation will occur. In a declarative language, a statement in the language specifies some aspect of the desired answer, with no notion of how that answer is to be determined. Admittedly, the issue is still likely cloudy. Additionally, as the level of abstraction of the nondeclarative languages increases and the aggressiveness of various compiler optimizations increases, the distinction is becoming less clear and likely of less interest.

Finally, let's consider language whose star is currently rising, Erlang. Erlang is a functional, strict, dynamically typed language with explicit language support for concurrent computation. All the other languages described here are sequential languages; although they can support concurrent execution by using threads or by adding a messaging layer, Erlang programs explicitly describe their concurrent execution and communicate explicitly through messages.

4.3   The Variety of Varieties

Just looking at these languages reveals categories related to the organizing principles of languages, their type systems, their execution behavior, and their implementation. There's something pretty important missing from this list, at least as it relates to general-purpose programming languages. Any language that supports conditional statements and indefinite iteration is considered Turing complete; all of these languages are capable of expressing any program that takes finite input and completes any task resulting in a finite output on that input in finite time.

So, what's the relevance of Turing completeness? Despite the passion with which people defend their preferred choice, all the major general-purpose programming languages, including Lisp, Ruby, Java, C#, C, and so on, and even the crusty old assembly languages, can express the same set of programs. Yes, I said the same set.

Now, just because you can write any program in any one of these languages doesn't mean it is always easy or desirable to do so. Different problems require different solutions; different languages provide different abstractions and techniques that facilitate these different solutions. The same algorithm implemented in different languages will obviously look quite different but will also possibly perform quite differently. One language may allow the algorithm to run more efficiently, for example. Another language may allow the algorithm to be more cleanly implemented. Compiler optimizations are more or less difficult depending on the language being compiled. Understanding the different languages characteristics and the programming models they support allows you to select the language appropriate for a particular task. Let's take these different aspects of variability and the options.

Paradigms

The set of programming paradigms generally includes imperative, procedural, functional, object-oriented, declarative, and logical. Some languages contain aspects of multiple paradigms. Common Lisp, for example, is a functional language supporting OO concepts as well. C++ has OO features but also has many features of procedural languages. The table on the next page shows the major programming paradigms:

Class	Definition	Examples
Imperative	Sequences of statements manipulate state.	Assembly, Fortran
Procedural	Organized around procedures—groups of statements.	C, Pascal, Cobol
Object-oriented	Organized around objects.	Smalltalk, Java, Ruby
Functional	Organized around stateless functions.	Lisp, Scheme, Haskell
Logical	Solution characteristics in terms of axioms and inference rules.	Prolog, OPS5
Declarative	Describes the solution, not how to achieve it.	XSLT, SQL, Prolog

This table might look like it combines things that aren't really much alike. Indeed, three different characteristics are wrapped up in this table.

There are notions of organization, state, and scoping. As described earlier, different language paradigms organize code differently, using objects, functions, procedures, or even single statements as the basic organizational unit. Then there is the notion of state. Imperative languages explicitly manipulate a memory state, whereas functional languages do not mutate any state. Finally, there is the notion of the visibility of state. In object-oriented languages, state resides in the object, and that state is visible only from the object itself. Imperative languages have a global state that is visible to all parts of a given program. Functional languages have bindings of variables to values within the closure of the function, but these are not mutable and are not visible to other functions.

Type Characteristics

The type of an identifier describes the legal values that identifier can hold and, implicitly, the operations that can be performed on that variable. There are several different kinds of type systems that refer to different types characteristics, but the most frequently discussed type characteristic describes when the type of a variable is determined. Statically typed languages assign a single type to a variable, often at compile time. In dynamically typed languages, the type of a variable is determined only when an operation is about to be performed on that variable. In such languages, the type of a given variable can potentially change over the execution of a problem; this cannot occur in statically typed languages. A particular style of dynamic typing utilized in Ruby, for instance, is *duck typing*. Under duck typing, the notion of the type of a value is weakened somewhat. The type of the value does not have to match a specific type; it merely needs to have the ability to perform the specifically requested operation.

Another important, although widely abused, term is *strongly typed*. A common definition for a strongly typed language is that a program is not allowed to compile if it might exhibit a type error at runtime. Of course, this then necessitates a definition-of-type error. Although division by zero, as an example, could be considered a type error, generally a type error is restricted to things like attempting an arithmetic operation on a string or an array.

One final aspect of typing that is of interest is type inference. Using type inference, the compiler attempts to infer a typing that renders the program correct. Type inference makes strongly typed languages more user friendly, although there are perfectly correct programs for which the type inference algorithms are unable to infer the correct type.

The following table shows some of the common languages and where they fall relative to these characteristics:

Class	Definition	Examples
Static	Type of a variable fixed, usually at compile time.	Java, C, Fortran, ...
Dynamic	Type of a variable determined when accessed.	Scheme, Lisp, Ruby
Strong	No runtime type errors are possible.	Haskell, C++ (if you ignore what you can do with casts)
Type Inference	A type inference algorithm assigns types to variables without explicit type definitions.	Haskell, ML
Duck Typing	Only the part of the type needed is checked.	Ruby

Execution Behavior

There are two different classes of behavior to discuss here, although there are many others that could be introduced. The first is the distinction between sequential and concurrent languages; the second is the distinction between lazy and strict languages.

Most programmers never think too much about concurrent computation, although even the advent of client-server models introduced some notion of concurrency. Given this, it isn't surprising that most languages are sequential; the execution semantics of the language assume that a single statement of the program at a time is executed. However, we've had access to parallel machines for decades, and many applications rely on parallel or distributed computation to perform their task. Sometimes this parallelism is inferred by the compiler. Other times, a messaging layer, a task layer, and possibly locking or semaphore libraries are used to introduce parallelism. Some languages include explicit language constructs to support parallelism. Although previously limited to applications in science research and complex financial analysis, such languages are coming into more mainstream consideration as multicore processors become more common and as the expectations of users of applications continue to expand.

Lazy evaluation is even less commonly thought about in business applications, but as interest in Haskell increases, the power of lazy evaluation will be better understood. Almost all languages have strict execution semantics. Simply put, this means statements are executed, in order, until the end of the program. Conceptually, lazy evaluation means that the execution begins by determining what the result is and finding which statements need to be executed to get that result. Any statement not directly required for the end result is ignored. Consider the following, admittedly silly, program in some unspecified language:

```
X = Y/0;
Y=6;
End(Y);
```

The end statement indicates that the desired final result is the value of Y. Under strict evaluation, this program would fail with a divide-by-zero exception (we'll ignore compiler optimizations here that remove dead code). Under lazy evaluation, even without compiler optimizations, this program would return the value 6. There is no need to determine the value of X, so that statement is ignored. The implications of lazy evaluation are further reaching than simply optimizations, allowing for the manipulation and specification of infinite data structures, for example; these implications are beyond the scope of this essay, though.

There's no need for a table here, since with the prominent exception of Haskell and the closely related Hope languages, most languages are strict. It is possible to implement lazy evaluation in a strict language for specific applications, but the language semantics remain strict.

Implementation Models

A final category of interest concerns how the language is implemented. There used to be two big, broadly understand categories: *compiled* and *interpreted* languages. In the "old days," interpreted languages were slow, so any real work needed to be done in compiled languages—or so the conventional wisdom went. Even in those days, people were writing real systems in Lisp, hard as that might be for some to believe. Interpreted languages were considered toy languages or simply scripting languages. The popularization of the virtual machine has blurred the line somewhat; as in languages such as Java, the program is compiled into some bytecode representation and then interpreted on the virtual machine. However, I still find the following distinction useful: a compiler creates something that needs to be executed to get an answer from some source program, whereas an interpreter takes some source program and actually produces an answer.

The phrase "scripting language" in particular seemed to convey that the language was worthy of writing scripts only rather than programs. The number of systems implemented in such languages tends to make that characterization seem rather silly.

Some languages, such as some versions of Scheme, have both compiled and interpreted versions, again clouding the characterizations.

Again, a table is less important here, because many languages exist in both compiled and interpreted versions and the use of bytecode-style virtual machines further complicates the issue.

4.4 The Tree of Life for Languages

The following table shows some common languages and where they fall relative to these categories. Many languages have quite similar characteristics, although the syntax may be very different. From the perspective of program design, the syntax is less relevant, because the expressiveness of the language derives more from its characteristics. However, individual programmers are generally picky about syntax; this makes sense given that they have to work directly with the syntax of a language. The resurgence of integrated development environments (IDEs) has lessened some of the syntactic burden, but it can never be eliminated.

Language	Paradigms	Typing	Implementation
Assembly	Imperative	Dynamic	Assembled, sequential
Fortran	Imperative	Static	Compiled, sequential with parallelizing compilers
C	Imperative, procedural	Static, but with pointers	Compiled, sequential
C++	Imperative, OO, procedural	Static, but with pointers	Compiled, sequential with parallelizing compilers
Java	Imperative, OO, procedural	Static	Compiled, with threads for concurrency
Lisp	Functional (CLOS adds OO) with some imperative	Dynamic	Interpreted and compiled, sequential
Scheme	Functional with some imperative	Dynamic	Interpreted and compiled, sequential
Haskell	Functional, lazy	Static, type inference	Interpreted and compiled
Ruby	OO	Dynamic, duck	Interpreted and compiled, sequential
Prolog	Declarative	Dynamic	
Scala	Functional and OO	Static	Interpreted and compiled, with parallel support
Erlang	Functional	Dynamic	Interpreted and compiled, concurrent

This list of categories is not exhaustive. We could discuss many different language features. Additionally, many features of older languages are beginning to appear in modern languages (closures, higher-order functions, and so on). Languages will continue to evolve to introduce new abstractions and approaches.

4.5 That's All Very Interesting, But Why Should You Care?

Language wars have been raging for decades, and there's no reason to believe they'll stop now. Some folks seem convinced that there is one perfect language out there. My belief is that this is simply hogwash. The notion is even more ridiculous if you accept that domain-specific languages (DSLs) will continue to gain popularity and if new approaches such as intentional programming and language workbenches really pan out. In reality, individual languages should have a set of features and syntax for those features that allows for the implementation of particular kinds of components or programs. Obviously, the broader a language's sweet spot, the more general purpose that language will be. Of course, from the perspective of a CIO with lots of applications to maintain, one true language would simplify matters of staffing tremendously, at least on the surface. We'll continue to argue over the relative merits of Java and Ruby or whatever the next set of contenders are. I can still dream, though, of a day when the discussion is about which language to use for a problem rather than just which language to use.

► In ten years, everyone will be programming in
Smalltalk, no matter what they call it.

Chapter 5

Polyglot Programming

by Neal Ford, Meme Wrangler

When Java came along in 1995, it was a welcome relief to C++ programmers tired of fighting with pointers, memory management, and
other arcane plumbing. Java allowed them to just get work done. But
for Java to succeed, it needed to appeal to the current high priesthood
of developers, those same C++ developers. Thus, the designers of Java
purposely made the Java language look and feel a lot like C++, which
made perfect sense. It's hard to attract developers to new languages if
they have to learn all the basics again.

But in 2008, backward compatibility no longer makes much sense.
Much of the strange stuff that new Java developers must learn has
nothing to do with getting real work done but rather with strange ritu-
als in Java. Think about the following code, which is the first code most
Java developers encounter:

```java
public class HelloWorld {
    public static void main(String[] args) {
        System.out.println("Hello, World");
    }
}
```

How many things do you have to explain to a new developer for them to
understand this code? Java is rife with C++-isms (such as zero-based
arrays) and baggage that made sense in 1995 (such as the distinction
between primitives and objects) that don't help the productivity of modern developers.

Fortunately, the designers of Java made a brilliant decision when they
built Java: they separated the *language* from the *platform*. That gives
developers a "get out of jail free" card called *polyglot programming*.

5.1 Polyglot Programming

The word *polyglot* means speaking many languages. Polyglot programming leverages the separation of language and platform in Java (and in C# as well), allowing developers to use specialized languages to solve specific problems. We now have hundreds of languages that run on the Java virtual machine and the .NET managed runtime. Yet, as developers, we don't leverage this capability enough.

Of course, developers already do this all the time: most applications use SQL to access databases, JavaScript to add interactivity to web pages, and of course the ubiquitous XML to configure everything. But the idea of polyglot programming is different. All these examples are orthogonal to the JVM; they run outside the world of Java. And that causes big headaches. How many billions of dollars have been spent on the impedance mismatch of objects and set-based SQL? Impedance mismatch makes developers nervous because they feel the pain of the places where they already use multiple languages. But polyglot programming is different. It is about leveraging languages that produce bytecode within the JVM, eliminating impedance mismatch.

The other impediment to polyglot programming is the perception that you are changing languages. Always in the past, changing languages meant changing platforms, which has an obvious bad connotation to developers who don't want to rewrite all their libraries again. But the separation of the platform from the language in both Java and C# means you no longer have to fight that battle. Polyglot programming allows you to leverage all your existing assets but also use languages more suitable to the job at hand.

Just what do I mean by more suitable to the job at hand? The following sections are some examples of applying polyglot programming.

5.2 Reading Files the Groovy Way

Here is a task: write a simple program that reads a text file and prints the contents of the text file with line numbers added to the front of each line. Here is the solution in Java:

`./code/ford/LineNumbers.java`

```
package com.nealford.polyglot.linenumbers;

import java.io.*;
import static java.lang.System.*;
```

```
public class LineNumbers {
    public LineNumbers(String path) {
        File file = new File(path);
        LineNumberReader reader = null;
        try {
            reader = new LineNumberReader(new FileReader(file));
            while (reader.ready()) {
                out.println(reader.getLineNumber() + ":"
                        + reader.readLine());
            }
        } catch (FileNotFoundException e) {
            e.printStackTrace();
        } catch (IOException e) {
            e.printStackTrace();
        } finally {
            try {
                reader.close();
            } catch (IOException ignored) {
            }
        }
    }

    public static void main(String[] args) {
        new LineNumbers(args[0]);
    }
}
```

Here is the same solution in Groovy, the scripting language that runs on the JVM:

./code/ford/LineNumbers.groovy

```
def number=0
new File (args[0]).eachLine { line ->
    number++
    println "$number: $line"
}
```

For simple tasks, Java is massively overcomplicated. In the previous example, there are more lines of boilerplate exception code than solution code. Groovy handles most of the mundane plumbing for you, making it easier to see the solution without all the ritual. This code compiles to Java bytecode, making the end result almost identical to the Java one. Yes, the bytecode for the Groovy version isn't going to be as efficient: Groovy has to do lots of magic with Java's bytecode to make it more dynamic (such as calling Java classes through proxy objects). But what's more important in this situation: developer productivity or efficiency of execution? If you are reading files to add line numbers and it takes 500 milliseconds vs. 100 milliseconds, who cares? You save several million times that amount in the time it saves you writing the code. Use the tool more suitable for the job rather than prematurely optimizing for performance.

5.3 JRuby and isBlank

Of course, the example in the previous section was a simple scripting solution for which Java is poorly suited. What about something more common, such as code you'd need in a web application to verify that parameters aren't blank?

This Java code comes from the Apache Commons project, which is a repository of commonly needed Java infrastructure code. It allows you to determine whether a String is blank, which comes up all the time in web application parameter harvesting. This is the isBlank() method from the StringUtils class:

./code/ford/StringUtils.java

```java
public static boolean isBlank(String str) {
    int strLen;
    if (str == null || (strLen = str.length()) == 0) {
        return true;
    }
    for (int i = 0; i < strLen; i++) {
        if ((Character.isWhitespace(str.charAt(i)) == false)) {
            return false;
        }
    }
    return true;
}
```

This code manages to expose lots of built-in deficiencies in the Java language. First, it's in a class called StringUtils, because the Java language won't allow you to make changes to or extend String. This is an example of a *poorly hung method*, meaning that it isn't part of the class it should be. Next, you must verify that the object sent to you isn't **null**. **null** is special in Java (it isn't a primitive or an object). Lots of Java code is required to check for nulls. Last, you must iterate over the string, making sure that all the remaining characters are whitespace. Of course, you can't call a method on each character to determine this (because characters are primitives); you must use the Character wrapper class.

Here is code that does the same thing in JRuby:

./code/ford/blankness.rb

```ruby
class String
  def blank?
    empty? || strip.empty?
  end
end
```

And here are tests to prove it:

./code/ford/test_blankness.rb

```ruby
require "test/unit"
require "blankness"

class BlankTest < Test::Unit::TestCase
  def test_blank
    assert "".blank?
    assert " ".blank?
    assert nil.to_s.blank?
    assert ! "x".blank?
  end

end
```

Notice several things about this solution. First, Ruby allows you to add methods directly to String, resulting in a property hung method. Second, the code is very simple because you don't have to worry about primitives vs. objects. Third, notice in the test that I don't have to worry about the nil case: nil in Ruby is an object (like everything else in the language), so if I try to pass a nil as a string, the to_s() method (Ruby's version of the toString() method) returns an empty string, which is blank.

You can't retrofit this code back into Java because the Java String class is final in the Java world. But, if you are using Ruby on Rails atop JRuby, you can do this with Java strings.

5.4 Jaskell and Functional Programming

Most of the examples presented so far deal with language deficiencies in Java. But polyglot programming also addresses fundamental design decisions. For example, threading is hard in imperative languages such as Java and C#. You must understand the nuances and side effects of using **synchronized** and how things are different when multiple threads access shared data.

With polyglot programming, you can avoid this issue entirely by using a functional language such as Jaskell (the Java version of Haskell) or Scala (a modern functional language written for the JVM).

Functional languages don't suffer many of the shortcomings of imperative languages. Functional languages adhere to mathematical principles more rigorously. For example, a function in a functional language works just like a function in mathematics: the output is entirely dependent on the input. In other words, functions can't modify external *state* as they do their work. When you call a mathematical function such as sin(), you don't worry that the next call to sin() might accidentally return the cosine because some internal state has been modified. Mathematical functions don't have internal state that can be modified between calls. Functions (and methods) in functional languages work the same way. Examples of functional languages include Haskell, O'Caml, SML, Scala, F#, and others.

In particular, functional languages handle multithreaded support much better than imperative languages because they discourage statefulness. The upshot of this is that it is easier to write robust thread-safe code in a functional language than in an imperative one.

Enter Jaskell. Jaskell is a version of the Haskell language that runs on the Java platform. In other words, it is a way to write Haskell code that produces Java bytecode.

Here is an example. Let's say you wanted to implement a class in Java that allowed safely accessing an element of an array. You could write a class that resembles the following:

./code/ford/SafeArray.java

```java
class SafeArray{
    private final Object[] _arr;
    private final int _begin;
    private final int _len;

    public SafeArray(Object[] arr, int len){
        _arr = arr;
        _begin = begin;
        _len = len;
    }

    public Object at(int i){
        if(i < 0 || i >= _len){
            throw new ArrayIndexOutOfBoundsException(i);
        }
        return _arr[_begin + i];
    }
}
```

```
    public int getLength(){
        return _len;
    }
}
```

You can write the same functionality in Jaskell as a *tuple*, which is essentially an associative array:

`./code/ford/safearray.jaskell`

```
newSafeArray arr begin len = {
  length = len;
  at i = if i < begin || i >= len then
           throw $ ArrayIndexOutOfBoundsException.new[i]
         else
           arr[begin + i];
}
```

Because tuples work as associative arrays, calling newSafeArray.at(3) calls the at portion of the tuple, which evaluates the code defined by that part of the tuple. Even though Jaskell isn't object-oriented, both inheritance and polymorphism can be simulated using tuples. And, some desirable behavior, such as *mixins*, is possible with tuples in Jaskell but not with the core Java language. Mixins offer an alternative to the combination of interfaces and inheritance, where you can inject code into a class, not just a signature, without using inheritance. Essentially, mixins give you polymorphism without inheritance.

Haskell (and therefore Jaskell) features lazy evaluation of functions, meaning that eventualities are never executed until needed. For example, this code is perfectly legal in Haskell but would never work in Java:

```
makeList = 1 : makeList
```

The code reads as "Make a list with a single element. If more elements are needed, evaluate them as needed." This function essentially creates a never-ending list of *1*s.

Perhaps you have a complex scheduling algorithm that would be 1,000 lines of Java code but only 50 of Haskell. Why not take advantage of the Java *platform* and write it in a language more suitable to the task? Increasingly, just as we have database administrators on projects, we will have other specialists to write some code that exhibits special characteristics.

It's unlikely that you'll write an entire application using solely Jaskell. But why not take advantage of what it does really well in your larger application? Let's say you have a web application that requires a highly concurrent scheduling piece. Write just the scheduling part in Jaskell, write the web pieces in Rails using JRuby (or Groovy on Grails), and leverage the existing code you've already written to communicate with your old mainframe. Because of the Java platform, you can glue them all together at the bytecode level, increasing your productivity because you are using tools better suited to the problems you need to solve.

5.5 Testing Java

Using multiple languages doesn't mean you have to throw out what you are already doing. Even in your existing infrastructure, you can leverage better-suited languages. One of the common tasks you need to perform is testing complex code. But creating mock object expectations can take a lot of time because Java isn't well suited to the flexibility required to allow objects to mimic others. Why not write the tests (and only the tests) in a more suitable language?

Here's an example of testing the interaction between an Order class (actually, class + interface) and a Warehouse class, using JMock (a popular mock object library for Java):

./code/ford/OrderInteractionTester.java

```
package com.nealford.conf.jmock.warehouse;

import org.jmock.Mock;
import org.jmock.MockObjectTestCase;

public class OrderInteractionTester extends MockObjectTestCase {
  private static String TALISKER = "Talisker";

  public void testFillingRemovesInventoryIfInStock() {
    //setup - data
    Order order = new OrderImpl(TALISKER, 50);
    Mock warehouseMock = new Mock(Warehouse.class);

    //setup - expectations
    warehouseMock.expects(once()).method("hasInventory")
      .with(eq(TALISKER),eq(50))
      .will(returnValue(true));
    warehouseMock.expects(once()).method("remove")
      .with(eq(TALISKER), eq(50))
      .after("hasInventory");

    //exercise
    order.fill((Warehouse) warehouseMock.proxy());
```

```
    //verify
    warehouseMock.verify();
    assertTrue(order.isFilled());
  }

}
```

This code tests that the Order class correctly interacts with the Warehouse class (through its interface), verifying that the proper methods are called and that the result is correct.

Here is the same test utilizing JRuby (and the powerful Mocha mock object library from the Ruby world) to perform the same test:

./code/ford/order_interaction_test.rb

```ruby
require 'test/unit'
require 'rubygems'
require 'mocha'

require "java"
require "Warehouse.jar"
%w(OrderImpl Order Warehouse WarehouseImpl).each { |f|
   include_class "com.nealford.conf.jmock.warehouse.#{f}"
 }

class OrderInteractionTest < Test::Unit::TestCase
  TALISKER = "Talisker"

  def test_filling_removes_inventory_if_in_stock
    order = OrderImpl.new(TALISKER, 50)
    warehouse = Warehouse.new
    warehouse.stubs(:hasInventory).with(TALISKER, 50).returns(true)
    warehouse.stubs(:remove).with(TALISKER, 50)

    order.fill(warehouse)
    assert order.is_filled
  end

end
```

This code is much more concise because Ruby is a dynamic language. You can directly instantiate an interface (in this case, Warehouse) because JRuby wraps Java objects in proxy classes. Also notice that you can put all the pertinent Java classes on the test's classpath with the simple require 'warehouse.jar' at the top. Wouldn't you love to be able to do that in Java?

Polyglot programming doesn't have to be a major, earth-moving switch in the way you work. In most companies, test code isn't considered "official" code, so you might not even need permission to start writing your tests in JRuby.

5.6 Polyglot Programming the Future

In early 2007, ThoughtWorks released its first-ever commercial product, called Mingle. It is an agile project-tracking tool. It was very important to achieve a fast time to market for Mingle, so we decided to write it in Ruby on Rails. But, we wanted to leverage some existing libraries that already existed, namely, Subversion support and a Java-based charting library. Thus, we implemented it using Rails on JRuby, which allowed us to use existing Java libraries and take advantage of the ease of deployment of Java. Mingle is the embodiment of this idea of polyglot programming: leveraging the best of tools for the job at hand while taking advantage of the robustness and richness of the underlying platform.

The days of trying to cram solutions into a single language are disappearing. Because we have outstanding managed runtimes (Java and CLR), we should leverage those platforms with better tools. Polyglot programming allows you to mix and match solutions without discarding all the code you already have that does important work. Language development is exploding on these two proven platforms. As developers, you need to learn how to take advantage of this growth so you can write better code using tools more suited to the job.

Chapter 6

Object Calisthenics

by Jeff Bay, Technology Principal

6.1   Nine Steps to Better Software Design Today

We've all seen poorly written code that's hard to understand, test, and maintain. Object-oriented programming promised to save us from our old procedural code, allowing us to write software incrementally, reusing as we go. But sometimes it seems like we're just chasing down the same old complex, coupled designs in Java that we had in C. This essay will give new programmers an opportunity to learn best practices while writing their own code. For sophisticated and experienced programmers, it will give you a vehicle to refocus on best practices or to use for demonstration purposes in teaching co-workers.

Good object-oriented design can be hard to learn; however, it can also result in immense gains in simplicity. Transitioning from procedural development to object-oriented design requires a major shift in thinking that is more difficult than it seems. Many developers assume they're doing a good job with OO design, when in reality they're unconsciously stuck in procedural habits that are hard to break. It doesn't help that many examples and best practices (even Sun's code in the JDK) encourage poor OO design in the name of performance or the simple weight of history.

The core concepts behind good design are well understood. As an example, here are seven code qualities that are commonly known to matter: cohesion, loose coupling, zero duplication, encapsulation, testability, readability, and focus. Yet it's hard to put those concepts into practice. It is one thing to understand that encapsulation means hiding data, implementation, type, design, or construction. It's another thing altogether to design code that implements encapsulation well. So here's an exercise that can help you internalize principles of good object-oriented design and actually use them in real life.

6.2 The Exercise

Do a simple project using far stricter coding standards than you've ever used in your life. In this essay, you'll find nine "rules of thumb" that will help push you into writing code that is almost required to be object-oriented. This will allow you to make better decisions and give you more and better options when confronted with the problems of your day job.

By suspending disbelief and rigidly applying these rules on a small, 1,000-line project, you'll start to see a significantly different approach to designing software. Once you've written 1,000 lines of code, the exercise is done, and you can relax and go back to using these rules as guidelines.

This is a hard exercise, especially because many of these rules are not universally applicable. The fact is that sometimes classes are little more than fifty lines. But there's great value in thinking about what would have to happen to move those responsibilities into real, first-class objects of their own. It's developing this type of thinking that's the real value of the exercise. So, stretch the limits of what you imagine is possible, and see whether you start thinking about your code in a new way.

The Rules

Here are the rules for the exercise:

1. Use only one level of indentation per method.
2. Don't use the else keyword.
3. Wrap all primitives and strings.
4. Use only one dot per line.
5. Don't abbreviate.
6. Keep all entities small.
7. Don't use any classes with more than two instance variables.
8. Use first-class collections.
9. Don't use any getters/setters/properties.

Rule 1: Use One Level of Indentation per Method

Ever stare at a big old method wondering where to start? A giant method lacks cohesiveness. One guideline is to limit method length to five lines, but that kind of transition can be daunting if your code is littered with 500-line monsters. Instead, try to ensure that each method does exactly one thing—one control structure or one block of statements per method. If you have nested control structures in a method, you're working at multiple levels of abstraction, and that means you're doing more than one thing.

As you work with methods that do *exactly* one thing, expressed within classes doing exactly one thing, your code begins to change. As each unit in your application becomes smaller, your level of reuse will start to rise exponentially. It can be difficult to spot opportunities for reuse within a method that has five responsibilities and is implemented in 100 lines. A three-line method that manages the state of a single object in a given context is usable in many different contexts.

Use the Extract Method feature of your IDE to pull out behaviors until your methods have only one level of indentation, like this, for example:

```
class Board {
        ...
        String board() {
                StringBuffer buf = new StringBuffer();
                for(int i = 0; i < 10; i++) {
                        for(int j = 0; j < 10; j++)
                                buf.append(data[i][j]);
                        buf.append("\n");
                }
                return buf.toString();
        }
}


Class Board {
        ...
        String board() {
                StringBuffer buf = new StringBuffer();
                collectRows(buf);
                Return buf.toString();
        }

        Void collectRows(StringBuffer buf) {
                For(int I = 0; I < 10; i++)
                        collectRow(buf, i);
        }
```

```
Void collectRow(StringBuffer buf, int row) {
        For(int I = 0; I < 10; i++)
                Buf.append(data[row][i]);
        buf.append("\n");
    }
}
```

Notice that another effect has occurred with this refactoring. Each individual method has become virtually trivial to match its implementation to its name. Determining the existence of bugs in these much smaller snippets is frequently much easier.

Here at the end of the first rule, I should also point out that the more you practice applying the rules, the more the advantages come to fruition. Your first attempts to decompose problems in the style presented here will feel awkward and likely lead to little gain that you can perceive. There is a skill to applying the rules, however; this is the art of the programmer raised to another level.

Rule 2: Don't Use the else Keyword

Every programmer understands the if/else construct. It is built into nearly every programming language, and simple conditional logic is easy for anyone to understand. Nearly every programmer has seen a nasty nested conditional that's impossible to follow or a case statement that goes on for pages. Even worse, it is all too easy to simply add another branch to an existing conditional rather than factoring to a better solution. Conditionals are also a frequent source of duplication. Status flags, for example, frequently lead to this kind of trouble:

```
public static void endMe() {
if (status == DONE) {
        doSomething();

} else {
        <other code>
        }
}
```

You have several options for rewriting this without the else. For simple cases, use this:

```
public static void endMe() {
        if (status == DONE) {
                doSomething();
                return;
        }
        <other code>
}
```

```
public static Node head() {
        if (isAdvancing()) { return first; }
        else { return last; }
}

public static Node head() {
        return isAdvancing() ? first : last;
}
```

Here, four lines have been collapsed down to one line with one extra word on it. Note that early returns can easily reduce clarity if overused. See the Design Patterns book [GHJV95] for the Strategy pattern to find an example of using polymorphism to avoid branching on the status inline. The Strategy pattern is particularly useful here if the branch on the status is duplicated in multiple places.

Object-oriented languages give you a powerful tool—polymorphism—for handling complex conditional cases. Simple cases can be replaced with guard clauses and early returns. Designs that use polymorphism can be easier to read and maintain and can express their intent more clearly. But it's not always easy to make the transition, especially when you have else in your back pocket. So as part of this exercise, you're not allowed to use else. Try the Null Object pattern; it may help in some situations. Other tools can help you rid yourself of the else as well. See how many alternatives you can come up with.

Rule 3: Wrap All Primitives and Strings

An int on its own is just a scalar with no meaning. When a method takes an int as a parameter, the method name needs to do all the work of expressing the intent. If the same method takes an hour as a parameter, it's much easier to see what's happening. Small objects like this can make programs more maintainable, since it isn't possible to pass a year to a method that takes an hour parameter. With a primitive variable, the compiler can't help you write semantically correct programs. With an object, even a small one, you are giving both the compiler and the programmer additional information about what the value is and why it is being used.

Small objects such as hour or money also give you an obvious place to put behavior that otherwise would have been littered around other classes. This becomes especially true when you apply the rule relating to getters and setters and only the small object can access the value.

Rule 4: Use Only One Dot per Line

Sometimes it's hard to know which object should take responsibility for an activity. If you start looking for lines of code with multiple dots, you'll start to find many misplaced responsibilities. If you have more than one dot on any given line of code, the activity is happening in the wrong place. Maybe your object is dealing with two other objects at once. If this is the case, your object is a middleman; it knows too much about too many people. Consider moving the activity into one of the other objects.

If all those dots are connected, your object is digging deeply into another object. These multiple dots indicate that you're violating encapsulation. Try asking that object to do something for you, rather than poking around its insides. A major part of encapsulation is not reaching across class boundaries into types that you shouldn't know about.

The Law of Demeter ("talk only to your friends") is a good place to start, but think about it this way: you can play with your toys, with toys that you make, and with toys that someone gives you. You don't ever, *ever* play with your toy's toys.

```
class Board {
    ...

    class Piece {
        ...
        String representation;
    }
    class Location {
        ...
        Piece current;
    }

    String boardRepresentation() {
        StringBuffer buf = new StringBuffer();
        for(Location l : squares())
            buf.append(l.current.representation.substring(0, 1));
        return buf.toString();
    }
}

class Board {
    ...

    class Piece {
        ...
        private String representation;
```

```
        String character() {
            return representation.substring(0, 1);
        }

        void addTo(StringBuffer buf) {
            buf.append(character());
        }
    }
    class Location {
        ...
        private Piece current;

        void addTo(StringBuffer buf) {
            current.addTo(buf);
        }
    }

    String boardRepresentation() {
        StringBuffer buf = new StringBuffer();
        for(Location l : squares())
            l.addTo(buf);
        return buf.toString();
    }
}
```

Note that in this example the algorithm's implementation details are more diffuse, which can make it a little harder to understand at a glance. However, you just create a named method for the piece's transformation into a character. This is a method with a strong cohesive name and job and is quite likely to be reused—the odds of representation.substring(0, 1)" being repeated in other parts of the program has now been reduced dramatically. The method names take the place of comments in this brave new world—spend time on those names. It really isn't more difficult to understand a program with this type of structure; it simply requires a slightly different approach.

Rule 5: Don't Abbreviate

It's often tempting to abbreviate in the names of classes, methods, or variables. Resist the temptation. Abbreviations can be confusing, and they tend to hide larger problems.

Think about why you want to abbreviate. Is it because you're typing the same word over and over again? If that's the case, perhaps your method is used too heavily, and you are missing opportunities to remove duplication. Is it because your method names are getting long? This might be a sign of a misplaced responsibility or a missing class.

Try to keep class and method names to one to two words, and avoid names that duplicate the context. If the class is an Order, the method doesn't need to be called shipOrder(). Simply name the method ship() so that clients call order.ship()—a simple and clear representation of what's happening.

For this exercise, all entities should have a name that is one or two words, with no abbreviations.

Rule 6: Keep All Entities Small

This means no class that's more than fifty lines and no package that's more than ten files.

Classes of more than fifty lines usually do more than one thing, which makes them harder to understand and harder to reuse. Fifty-line classes have the added benefit of being visible on one screen without scrolling, which makes them easier to grasp quickly.

What's challenging about creating such small classes is that there are often groups of behaviors that make logical sense together. This is where you need to leverage packages. As your classes become smaller and have fewer responsibilities and as you limit package size, you'll start to see that packages represent clusters of related classes that work together to achieve a goal. Packages, like classes, should be cohesive and have a purpose. Keeping those packages small forces them to have a real identity.

Rule 7: Don't Use Any Classes with More Than Two Instance Variables

Most classes should simply be responsible for handling a single state variable, but a few will require two. Adding a new instance variable to a class immediately decreases the cohesion of that class. In general, while programming under these rules, you'll find that there are two kinds of classes, those that maintain the state of a single instance variable and those that coordinate two separate variables. In general, don't mix the two kinds of responsibilities.

The discerning reader might have noticed that rules 3 and 7 can be considered to be isomorphic. In a more general sense, there are few cases where a cohesive single job description can be created for a class with many instance variables.

Here's an example of the kind of dissection I'm asking you to engage in:

```
    String first;
    String middle;
    String last;
}
```

The previous code could be decomposed into two classes like this:

```
class Name {
    Surname family;
    GivenNames given;
}

class Surname {
    String family;
}

class GivenNames {
    List<String> names;
}
```

Note that in thinking about how to do the decomposition, the opportunity to separate the concerns of a family name (used for many legal entity restrictions) could be separated from an essentially different kind of name. The GivenName object here contains a list of names, allowing the new model to absorb people with first, middle, and other given names. Frequently, the decomposition of instance variables leads to an understanding of commonality of several related instance variables. Sometimes several related instance variables actually have a related life in a first-class collection.

Decomposing objects from a set of attributes into a hierarchy of collaborating objects leads much more directly to an effective object model. Prior to understanding this rule, I spent many hours trying to follow data flows through large objects. It was possible to tweeze out an object model, but it was a painstaking process to understand the related groups of behavior and see the result. In contrast, the recursive application of this rule has led to a very quick decomposition of complex large objects into much simpler models. Behavior naturally follows the instance variables into the appropriate place—the compiler and the rules on encapsulation won't allow otherwise. If you get stuck, work downward by splitting objects into related halves or upward by picking any two instance variables and making an object out of them.

Rule 8: Use First-Class Collections

The application of this rule is simple: any class that contains a collection should contain no other member variables. Each collection gets wrapped in its own class, so now behaviors related to the collection have a home. You may find that filters become part of this new class. Filters may also become function objects in their own right. Also, your new class can handle activities such as joining two groups together or applying a rule to each element of the group. This is an obvious extension of the rule about instance variables but is important for its own sake as well. A collection is really a type of very useful primitive. It has many behaviors but little semantic intent or clues for either the next programmer or the maintainer.

Rule 9: Don't Use Any Getters/Setters/Properties

The last sentence of the previous rule leads almost directly to this rule. If your objects are now encapsulating the appropriate set of instance variables but the design is still awkward, it is time to examine some more direct violations of encapsulation. The behavior will not follow the instance variable if it can simply ask for the value in its current location. The idea behind strong encapsulation boundaries is to force programmers working on the code after you leave it to *look for* and *place* behavior into a single place in the object model. This has many beneficial downstream effects, such as a dramatic reduction in duplication errors and a better localization of changes to implement new features.

This rule is commonly stated as "Tell, don't ask."

6.3 Conclusion

Eight of these nine rules are simply ways to visualize and implement the Holy Grail of object-oriented programming—the encapsulation of data. In addition, another drives the appropriate use of polymorphism (not using else and minimizing all conditional logic), and another is a naming strategy that encourages concise and straightforward naming standards, without inconsistently applied and hard-to-pronounce abbreviations.

The entire thrust is to craft code that has no duplication in code or idea. The goal is code that concisely expresses simple and elegant abstractions for the incidental complexity we deal with all day long.

In the long run, you will inevitably find that these rules contradict each other in some situations or that applying the rules leads to degenerate results. For the purpose of the exercise, however, spend 20 hours and 1,000 lines writing code that conforms 100% to these rules. You will find yourself having to break old habits and change rules that you may have lived with for your whole programming life. Each of the rules has been chosen such that if you follow it, you will encounter situations that would typically have an obvious (but perhaps incorrect) answer that is not available to you.

Following these rules with discipline will force you to come up with the harder answers that lead to a much richer understanding of object-oriented programming. If you write 1,000 lines that follow all these rules, you will find that you have created something completely different from what you expected. Follow the rules, and see where you end up. If you keep working at it, the code you are writing might conform to these rules without any conscious effort on your part.

On a final note, some might see these rules as overkill or impossible to apply in a real working system. They would be incorrect—I'm finalizing a system as this book goes to press that has more than 100,000 lines written in this style. The programmers working on this system routinely follow these rules and are each overjoyed to see how much less tiresome development can be when embracing deep simplicity.

Chapter 7

What Is an Iteration Manager Anyway?

by Tiffany Lentz, Project Manager

As the industry changes and buzzwords such as *agile*, *iterative*, and *iteration* become more commonplace, a new and ambiguously defined role has emerged: iteration manager. Is this the project manager for the new generation? Is this a glorified team lead? Is this a new layer of management? Who is this masked manager?

This essay highlights the function and value of having an iteration manager as a member of a software team. We'll look at the limits of an iteration manager's responsibilities and discuss how iteration managers play an integral role in maintaining a healthy environment amidst organizational and cultural challenges.

7.1 What Is an Iteration Manager?

In general, on a large agile project, the project manager cannot focus on the success of each iteration for any specific project team and the entire program at the same time. When teams were struggling to find high-priority work to do on one particular project in 2000, the solution was to identify someone who could provide a continual stream of high-priority functionality at a sustainable pace to the delivery teams. This is the role that has grown into the iteration manager (IM).

In an iterative development world, someone needs to support the team, facilitate daily conversations with the business customer, and keep the team focused on the top-priority efforts. Fred George, senior architect at

ThoughtWorks, describes the iteration manager as "the inward-facing role for the management team. The iteration manager is responsible for the smooth flow of stories through the team. This includes creating sound team assignments and recommending staff changes as skill needs shift."

7.2 What Makes a Good Iteration Manager?

IMs can come from many different skill backgrounds—they can be technical (with strong people skills!), they can be analytical (with strong people skills!), or they can come from any number of other business or administrative specialties (with strong people skills!). They must have a forward-thinking, can-do attitude and an aptitude that embraces change. These inward-facing facilitators use their aptitude to perfect the processes of their delivery team on a daily basis.

For instance, once an iteration's workload is agreed upon, the IM tracks the team's progress throughout the course of the iteration and pragmatically and proactively implements process improvement changes within the team. Imagine that in a daily stand-up meeting, the IM hears a developer mention that he has been working for three days on a story that was estimated to be completed in one day. Since the IM is responsible for each team member's daily activities and for the iteration's progress, the IM should begin digging further into the details of this underestimated story. If the IM does not quickly determine the actual status of the story and communicate any implications of change in the iteration schedule to the customer immediately, the team will be at risk of missing its commitment. The IM could begin by asking the following questions:

- Does the developer understand the scope of the story?
- Have the story's tasks changed since the original estimate, and if so, how?
- Does the developer need help from the business analyst or customer to better understand the desired end state of the story?
- Does the developer need help from the technical lead?
- Is something standing in the developer's way of getting the story done (in other words, is it a hardware, software, or infrastructure problem)?
- Is the developer allocated to another project or attending too many miscellaneous meetings to get the story done?

These questions are just an example of how an IM might work to keep the team on schedule and communicate the daily status to the customer. The IM must be listening and responding to the team's needs every day. The primary responsibility of an IM is to develop a well-oiled machine that can deliver functionality, at a desired quality, within project boundaries.

IMs should have technical familiarity balanced with business knowledge. Mary and Tom Poppendieck write that agile leaders have "a deep understanding of both the customers and the technical issues that gains them the respect of the development team." Good communication skills are a necessity. IMs function as the team's advocate in the relationship with the customers and the relationship with management.

Also, the IM must facilitate, enforce, and defend the team member's *rights*. For many agile teams, these rights come from the developers' Bill of Rights. These rights are agreed upon by the entire team, and often the team needs the assistance of the IM to ensure that they are enforced.

Often this takes the shape of facilitating intrateam and interteam communication. Most developers are not accustomed to talking directly to the customer and getting their direct input on story completion. The IM often needs to facilitate open communication by providing examples of metrics, charts, and graphs.

The IM must uphold the customer's rights, too. Every time the temptation of team members to work out of priority order rears its ugly head, the IM steps in as the customer advocate. The customer has the right to pay for work in their desired priority order, remember? Throughout all this, the IM must remain a neutral party.

7.3 What an Iteration Manager Is Not

An IM is not a project manager (PM). Unlike a PM, the IM is engaged on the ground with the team members during their day-to-day activities. If you're an IM, leave the budgeting, resource managing, compliance, and general mayhem to the PM. Just focus on the team!

Further, an IM is a team member and not a people or resource manager. The IM cannot be responsible for writing a yearly review of team members. This would undermine their central task of remaining a neutral party who can defend the team while keeping the team focused on the customers' highest-priority functionality. Team members should not be more concerned with giving the IM a good impression than with asking for help when they need it.

The IM is also not the customer. Often the team's business analysts or the architect may function as the customer, depending on the nature of the stories or the availability of the actual customer. However, the IM should never function as the customer. The IM cannot facilitate proper problem solving with the team if they are making decisions as a customer.

Finally, an IM typically does not ensure technical integrity, ensure adherence to standards, or provide technical infrastructure support (for the build, deployment, or databases, for example). Project fulfillment activities such as coordinating across projects and coordinating deployment or rollout usually fall to the technical lead or lead business analyst.

7.4 The Iteration Manager and the Team

The iteration manager role, while not prescriptive, entails several daily responsibilities. Some of these are as follows:

- Collects time spent on stories
- Makes bottlenecks in the delivery process visible
- Reports team status to the customer
- Addresses issues, impediments, and obstacles raised at the daily stand-up meeting
- Controls all work flowing into the team and manages the distribution of that work to maintain a sustainable pace

Many metrics can be generated from collecting actual hours spent on individual stories. Gathering these hours to compare them to various other data points helps the IM sharpen the team's output. First, comparing the actual hours spent on completed stories to the number of story points completed within an iteration allows the IM to know what percentage of the team's time is being spent on actual story delivery, as opposed to team meetings, and so on. Second, comparing the actual hours spent on completed stories to the team's planned time for the project gives the IM an idea of team capacity and how available the team is to the project. Finally, comparing the actual hours spent on completed stories to story estimates produces estimation accuracy. All of these metrics are useful in different environments and should be used to help the team find a consistent delivery pace.

This consistent delivery pace is the basis for calculating team capacity for future iterations. By capturing the team's completely tested output of each iteration and capturing the planned availability of each team member, the IM can plan capacity for delivery based on actual, proven data. Capacity is not dictated for the team or picked based on a need to deliver at a specific time. Capacity is calculated so the team members govern themselves. If the pace is not in line with the business need, other project levers can be adjusted, but the actual output continues to predict the future capacity.

Bottlenecks can be identified by several metrics or careful layout of a story card wall. Noting that a story estimated at one day is still sitting in the development category on the story card wall after three days effectively highlights a bottleneck that opens team discussion. One successful metric created by Fred George is the *finger chart*. This chart uses a stacked area graph, with each area representing each of the phases in the delivery life cycle. Updating the story status daily allows the team to watch each area on the graph grow and watch the stories flow through the delivery life cycles. When all the areas on the graph are growing proportionately, the areas resemble fingers. When one area on the graph is out of proportion compared to the others (that is, the Awaiting Development area is wider than the Development area), a bottleneck appears. At this point, the team can discuss how to reduce the bottleneck to restabilize the team's delivery pace.

During the daily stand-up meeting, the IM removes noise and keeps the team members on track as they give their update of what they did the past twenty-four hours, what they will do the next twenty-four hours, and what their impediments are. The IM listens for action items and obstacles to remove that day so the team members can complete their story cards. If the IM hears someone monopolizing time in the daily stand-up meeting for more than the standard update, the IM can bring the team back to focus. This usually means suggesting that the person with a larger issue address it following the meeting.

7.5 The Iteration Manager and the Customer

As already discussed, metrics help the IM determine the team's sustainable pace. This allows the team to regularly make commitments and keep them. However, in order for the team members to uphold their commitments, the IM must keep the customer from changing the stories during the iteration. The IM acts as a gatekeeper, helping the customer prioritize upcoming work without distracting the team by constantly changing priorities.

As the gatekeeper, the IM protects the team from distraction and protects the customer from inadvertently hurting the team's productivity. Outside the iteration, customers can and should change priorities constantly. Until an iteration starts, all decision-making factors are subject to change, and new information is regularly introduced.

The concept of just-in-time decision making within a project is not a new one. The Lean Development System as implemented by Toyota's Knowledge-Based Engineering has been successfully employing a technique called Set-Based Concurrent Engineering for years. Set-Based Concurrent Engineering is described as "being very careful not to make decisions until they absolutely must be made and working hard to maintain options so that decisions can be made as late as possible with the most amount of information possible to allow the development team to arrive at a more optimal solution much faster than an approach that closes off options quickly for the sake of being *decisive*."

7.6 The Iteration Manager and the Iteration

There are also iteration-specific responsibilities. The IM works with the customer and team to plan each iteration by:

- Helping the customer prioritize
- Facilitating the team's recommendations
- Planning the team's capacity for delivery

The IM coaches, encourages, and motivates the team. The IM keeps the team honest by performing health checks. These checks are not to assure that the team is true to all components of agile but to see which techniques agile offers from which the team might benefit.

One final iteration-specific responsibility resting on the IM's shoulders is meeting facilitation. The IM owns and conducts planning meetings, including the iteration planning meetings and the release planning meetings. Proper facilitation of the iteration planning meetings and release planning meetings sets the team up for success. Metrics, what's working, and what's not as well as capacity planning all must be discussed openly and honestly.

During the release planning meetings, the IM shows their strength as a visionary by working with the customer to plan high-level pieces of functionality to be delivered for the next release. Once this has been agreed upon and the expectation set that it will change, the IM helps the team add high-level estimates (for example, story points) to give the customer an idea of what can be delivered in the next release.

Within the iteration planning meeting, the iteration manager often protects the team members from themselves as they sign up for more work than they can deliver. Also, by reviewing the metrics, the IM helps the team members "own" their tools and improve their output.

Finally, the IM facilitates the retrospective, so the team can "fail fast" and make visible the improvements needed during the next iteration. The IM leads the team's discussion concerning what is working and not working during the iteration. Through this discussion, opportunities arise to assign team members to focus on improving the things that are not working. This creates a circle of accountability that empowers the team members to better themselves.

7.7 The Iteration Manager and the Project

As discussed in this essay, an IM has a typical set of project-related responsibilities, but occasionally they are called on to meddle in cultural objectives within their teams. IMs facilitate an environment that creates fulfilled, happy, productive, and respected team members while satisfying business customers. Fred George said, "As a secondary objective, I look for the iteration manager to give back better people at the end of the project. The team is a sacred trust, and broadening their skills is the job of the iteration manager."

IMs should work toward a professional and accountable environment. Such environments exhibit proper behaviors and mannerisms, such as the following:

- Mutual respect is displayed for self, others, and customers.
- Successes are celebrated.
- Mistakes are treated as learning experiences.

The iteration manager strives to form the team into one cohesive group, where members succeed and fail together.

7.8 Conclusion

Building a well-oiled delivery machine, continually feeding it story cards, and tuning the machine all constitute a full-time job. Articulate communication, pragmatism, and an aptitude for change are difficult skills to find and develop. Since 2000, ThoughtWorks has trained IMs and sent them to clients, increasing and stabilizing the success of agile projects. IMs leave behind a repeatable process to enhance agile teams, complete projects within set boundaries, and improve team cultures. This results in happy, productive team members.

Having daily communication, removing noise, and keeping the customer up-to-date can fill up a developer's day with little time left to write code. Without an iteration manager on an agile team, the team is likely to fail. The team needs to remain focused on the task (or story) at hand and leave the noise to the iteration manager.

Chapter 8

Project Vital Signs

by Stelios Pantazopoulos, Iteration Manager

In the field of medicine, a doctor or nurse can walk into a patient's room, look at the patient's chart, and get a near real-time summary of the patient's vital signs. With that information in hand, the practitioner can quickly form an opinion of the patient's health and decide whether corrective action is necessary.

Wouldn't it be great for a custom software development project to have a chart, like the one a medical practitioner has, that would give a near real-time summary of the project's vital signs?

This essay proposes simple, pragmatic, low-overhead approaches for capturing a near real-time summary of a project's vital signs and to effectively communicate those vital signs to the project team members and stakeholders. In this way, the team has information to make an informed opinion about the health of the project and to propose corrective action to address the root cause of the project's health problems.

8.1 Project Vital Signs

Project vital signs are quantitative metrics that, taken collectively, give timely insights into overall project health.

Project vital signs include the following:

- *Scope burn-up*: The state of scope delivery for a deadline
- *Delivery quality*: The state of the end product being delivered
- *Budget burn-down*: The state of the budget in terms of scope delivery

- *Current state of implementation*: The real-time state of the system delivery
- Team perceptions: The team perspective on the state of the project

8.2 Project Vital Signs vs. Project Health

Project vital signs are independent metrics that should not be confused with project health. Project health is an opinion of the overall state of the project that is formed from an analysis of the project vital signs. By its very nature, project health is subjective and not measurable. When looking at the same project vital signs, two project team members could arrive at different conclusions regarding project health. A manager might place more weight on budget burn-down, while QA might put more emphasis on delivery quality. Developers might consider scope burn-up more significant. An opinion on project health has much to do with each team member's perspective. Regardless, each opinion is relevant, important, and unique.

The best way for team members to arrive at an informed opinion of overall project health is to collect and publish project vital signs. Without project vital signs as a frame of reference, an opinion of project health is little more than a guess.

Each team needs to create its own definition of project health. To form a consensus on project health, the team members must produce a list of project vital signs about which they will want information. Once they have identified project vital signs, then they need to develop information radiators for those project vital signs.

8.3 Project Vital Signs vs. Information Radiator

An *information radiator*, a term coined by Alistair Cockburn, is a "publicly posted display that shows people walking by what is going on." Information radiators are an effective approach to communicating project vital signs.

There is no single "must-have" information radiator for a project vital sign. This essay suggests one for each project vital sign that has proven effective for practitioners. The information radiators that follow are not the only way to communicate the project vital signs, however.

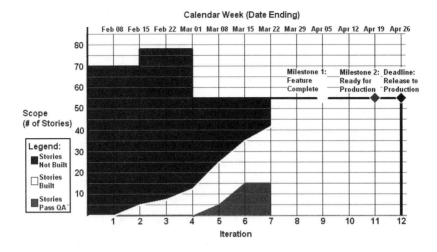

Figure 8.1: SCOPE BURN-UP CHART

8.4 Project Vital Sign: Scope Burn-Up

Scope burn-up represents the state of scope delivery for a deadline. Metrics should illustrate the amount of scope, the rate at which scope is delivered, and the deadline for scope delivery.

Example Information Radiator for Scope Burn-Up

The scope burn-up chart shown in Figure 8.1 is an approach for measuring and communicating how much of the system has been built and how much remains to be built.

Information conveyed by the chart includes the following:

- The unit of measure for scope (the number of stories)
- The total scope as measured at the end of each week (fifty-five stories as of March 22)
- The interim milestones important to the successful delivery of the scope (milestones 1 and 2)
- The week-by-week progress toward the interim milestones (fifteen of the fifty-five stories in scope are production-ready as of March 22)
- The deadline for the delivery of the scope (April 26, the end of iteration 12)

To facilitate communication, visibility, and ease of maintenance, the chart should be managed by a development lead or iteration manager and exist on a white board located in proximity to the entire project team.

Defining a Unit of Measure for Scope

To effectively capture scope burn-up, all project team members must agree to a unit of measure for defining the scope. Invariably, the definition of the unit of measure for the scope will vary depending on the project. Ideally, the definition of the unit of measure does not change during the course of the project. If the definition changes midstream, historical scope burn-up data in most cases becomes unusable.

Avoid using hours (or days) as a unit of measure for the scope. The scope is meant to be a measurement of how much there is to do, not a length of time (that is, it should be how much, not how long). With time comes the associated baggage of estimated time vs. actual time, thus making it more difficult to effectively measure and communicate scope.

Using Interim Milestones to Uncover Bottlenecks

The rate of progress toward interim milestones indicates how well the delivery process works. Delivery bottlenecks can be uncovered by comparing rates of progress toward interim milestones. A difference between rates indicates a delivery bottleneck. For example, a bottleneck in the QA feedback loop is apparent when the rate of progress to the Feature Complete milestone is greater than for the Ready for Production milestone.

Scope Burn-up Chart Further Explained

For the project described in the scope burn-up chart, the unit of measure for the scope is stories.

For this example, the team arrived at a definition for the story unit of measure prior to project inception.

The team defined a *story* as having the following characteristics:

- It represents all or part of the implementation of one or more use cases.
- A developer can build and unit test its implementation in two to five calendar days.
- Quality assurance can acceptance test its implementation to ensure it meets the requirements.

In this example, two interim milestones for the implementation of the scope were defined and set at the start of the project. Milestone 1 was the expected date to have all stories built and unit tested but not yet passed Quality Assurance. Milestone 2 was the date when all stories are expected to be built and unit tested and to have passed Quality Assurance. Progress toward the successful completion of the interim milestones was tracked directly in the project burn-up chart.

This is a brief explication of how the project managed scope:

1. At the start of the project, the scope was seventy stories.
2. During iteration 2, eight stories were added to the scope, bringing the total to seventy-eight stories.
3. During iteration 4, all project stakeholders met and came to the consensus that, given historical trends in the project burn-up chart, the team was unlikely to hit milestones 1 and 2 on time, on budget, and with the desired quality. The agreed course of action was to cut the scope. In a subsequent meeting, the stakeholders agreed to postpone twenty-three stories to a future release, thus bringing the scope down to fifty-five stories.
4. For iteration 5, the scope was decreased to fifty-five stories.
5. The project is currently in iteration 8. The scope is still at fifty-five stories. The team members are unsure of whether they will meet milestone 2, but they have decided to hold back on taking any corrective action at this time.

These are the raw scope metrics that went into producing the scope burn-up chart metrics:

Iteration	Scope	On Deck or In Development	Built and Awaiting QA	Built But Has Serious Bugs	Built and Passes QA
1	70	70	0	0	0
2	78	73	2	3	0
3	78	71	1	6	0
4	78	66	3	9	0
5	55	25	9	11	10
6	55	20	8	12	15
7	55	13	10	17	15

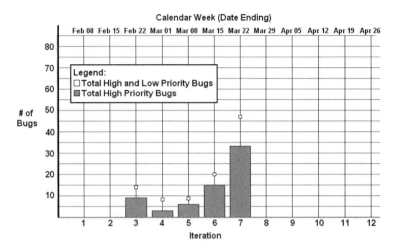

Figure 8.2: Bug count chart

8.5 Project Vital Sign: Delivery Quality

The delivery quality represents the state of the end product being delivered. Metrics should illustrate how well the team delivers on the scope.

Example Information Radiator for Quality

The bug count chart (shown in Figure 8.2) is an approach to measuring and communicating the number of system defects grouped by severity.

The chart conveys the following information:

- The total count of bugs yet to be resolved (forty-seven bugs as of the week of March 22, the end of iteration 7)
- The count of bugs that must be fixed before release (high-priority bug section; thirty-three of the forty-seven bugs as of the week of Mar 22, the end of iteration 7)
- The count of bugs whose fix could be postponed to a future release (low-priority bug section; fourteen of the forty-seven bugs as of the week of March 22, the end of iteration 7)
- Week-by-week historical bug counts (zero at the end of iterations 1 and 2; fourteen at the end of iteration 3; eight at end of iteration 4; nine at end of iteration 5; and twenty at end of iteration 6)

To facilitate communication, visibility, and ease of maintenance, the chart should be managed by Quality Assurance and exist on a white board in proximity to the entire project team.

Bug Count Chart Further Explained

When submitting a bug report, Quality Assurance assigns a severity level to the bug of either Low, Medium, High, or Critical. Critical bugs hold back Quality Assurance and must be fixed immediately. High bugs must be fixed before release to production. Medium bugs should ideally have a fix in place before release to production. Low bugs are ones that would be nice to fix but are not essential repairs.

On Monday mornings, the Quality Assurance team updates the bug count chart to include bug counts as they were reported as of the end of day Friday. High-priority bugs are all outstanding bugs with a severity rating of Critical or High. Low-priority bugs are all the outstanding bugs with a severity level of Medium or Low.

In this project example, bug counts were zero for the first two weeks because the Quality Assurance team was not yet assembled and no one was acceptance testing the story implementations built to date.

The following are the raw bug count metrics that went into producing the chart:

Last Day of Iteration	Critical Bug Count	High Bug Count	Medium Bug Count	Low Bug Count
1	0	0	0	0
2	0	0	0	0
3	0	9	4	1
4	0	3	4	1
5	0	6	2	1
6	0	15	3	2
7	3	30	10	4

8.6 Project Vital Sign: Budget Burn-Down

Budget burn-down represents the state of the budget in terms of scope delivery. Metrics illustrate how much budget the project has, the rate at which the budget is spent, and how long the budget needs to last.

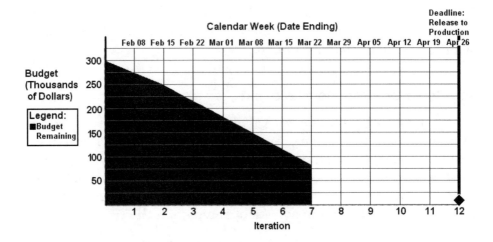

Figure 8.3: BUDGET BURN-DOWN CHART

Example Information Radiator for Budget

The budget burn-down chart is an approach for measuring and communicating the amount of project budget spent, the amount of budget remaining, and the rate the budget is spent. An example is shown in Figure 8.3.

The chart conveys the following information:

- The unit of measure for the budget (in thousands of dollars)
- The total budget (fixed at $300,000 at the start)
- The budget spent to date (budget spent section; $220,000 spent by end of iteration 7)
- The budget remaining to date (budget remaining section; $80,000 remaining at end of iteration 7)
- Week-by-week burn-down of budget ($25,000 per week for iterations 1 and 2; grows to $33,333 per week from iteration 3 forward)
- Deadline for delivery of the scope (April 26, the end of iteration 12)

To facilitate communication, visibility, and ease of maintenance, the chart should be managed by the project manager and exist on a white board in proximity to the entire project team.

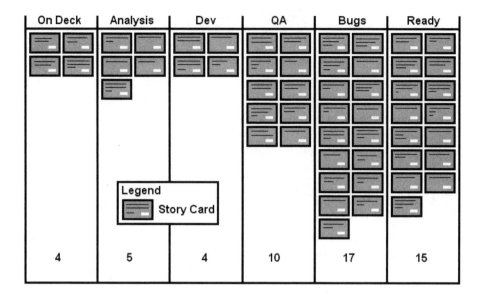

Figure 8.4: STORYBOARD

Budget Burn-Down Chart Further Explained

For iterations 1 and 2 of the project, there were eight billable project team members, each with a leased workstation and one leased development build/source control server shared by all. The weekly budget burn-down for the billable team members, leased workstations, and leased server was $25,000.

In iteration 3, two billable team members, two leased workstations, and one leased acceptance test server were added to the project. The increase in billable team members, leased workstations, and leased servers resulted in an increase in the weekly budget burn-down to $33,333.

8.7 Project Vital Sign: Current State of Implementation

The current state of implementation represents the real-time state of the system delivery. Metrics should illustrate the real-time state of delivery of each item within the scope.

Figure 8.5: STORY CARD

Example of an Information Radiator for Current State of Implementation

The storyboard (shown in Figure 8.4, on the previous page) and the story card (shown in Figure 8.5) are approaches to measuring and communicating the state of the system's implementation at the present time. The chart and cards convey the following information:

- Each item that encompasses the scope (all fifty-five stories in scope, with each represented as a gray story card)
- The states of implementation that an item can be in (On Deck, Analysis, Dev, QA, Bugs, and Ready)
- The current state of implementation of each item in scope (each story card is filed under a state of implementation)
- The number of items at each state of implementation (four on Deck, five in Analysis, four in Dev, ten in QA, seventeen in Bugs, fifteen in Ready)
- The developer currently assigned to the implementing the item (the yellow sticky note with the developer name on the story card; John is assigned to story 35)

To facilitate visibility, communication, and ease of maintenance, the board should be managed by analysts, developers, and Quality Assurance and exist on a white board in proximity to the entire project team.

Defining States of Implementation

The states of implementation that an item can be in are unique to each project. The states, as put forward in Figure 8.4, on the previous page, do not necessarily make sense for all projects. The states decided upon should be clearly understood and agreed upon by all members of the team.

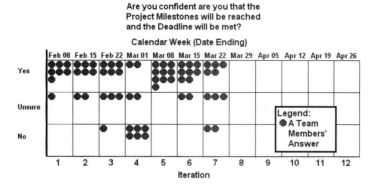

Figure 8.6: TEAM MOOD CHART

Changing the states of implementation midproject is acceptable. Often the states of implementation have to be revisited midproject because, in hindsight, the original ones no longer make sense.

Storyboard and Story Card Further Explained

The storyboard is as of 3:14 p.m. on the Tuesday of iteration 8. This is a further description of each state of implementation:

State of Implementation	Definition
On Deck	Story analysis and implementation has yet to begin.
Analysis	Story analysis is in progress.
Dev	Story construction and unit test is in progress.
QA	Story implementation is built, unit tested, and now ready for review by Quality Assurance.
Bugs	Quality Assurance has reviewed the story and found problems with its implementation.
Ready	Quality Assurance has reviewed the story implementation, and the problems identified with it have been fixed.

8.8 Project Vital Sign: Team Perceptions

Team perceptions are the collective team perspective on the state of the project. Metrics should illustrate the team's opinion of a certain aspect of project delivery.

Example of an Information Radiator for Team Perceptions

The team mood chart (shown in Figure 8.6, on the preceding page) is an approach to measuring and communicating team members' perceptions of how the project is progressing.

The chart conveys the following information:

- Questions asked to team members at each weekly iteration retrospective meeting ("Are you confident...?")
- The possible answers to the question that team members could give ("yes," "unsure," or "no")
- The answers each team member gave to the question asked ("When asked at the iteration 6 retrospective meeting, eight of ten team members answered yes")

To facilitate visibility, communication, and ease of maintenance, the chart should be updated by all team members at a weekly retrospective meeting and exist on a white board in proximity to the entire project team. The answers of the team members should be submitted anonymously in an attempt to circumvent influence or intimidation by other team members.

A team is not restricted to having only one question.

Team Mood Chart Further Explained

Each team member's answer to the question is represented by a green dot. Answers to the question are submitted anonymously at a weekly retrospective meeting.

In this project, the number of project team members has changed since project inception. For iterations 1 and 2, there were eight team members. For iteration 3 and on, there were ten team members.

Chapter 9

Consumer-Driven Contracts: A Service Evolution Pattern

by Ian Robinson, Architect[1]

Service-oriented architectures (SOAs) increase organizational agility and reduce the overall cost of change. Placing high-value business functions in discrete, reusable services makes it easier to connect and orchestrate them to satisfy core business processes. The cost of change is further reduced by decreasing the dependencies between services so that they can be rapidly recomposed and tuned in response to change or unplanned events.

A business can fully realize these benefits, however, only if its SOA enables services to evolve independently of one another. The commonly accepted way of enabling this independence is to build services that share contracts, not types. Providers publish a contract that describes the service, the messages it sends and receives, its endpoints, and the accepted ways of communicating with it. Consumers can thereafter implement the contract and use the service without any ties either to the internal domain representations maintained by the service or to the platform and technologies on which it is based.

In this essay, I'll discuss how service contracts and the ways they are often implemented and consumed can lead to overly coupled services. Developing services against contracts can quite often force us to evolve

1. I would like to thank the following individuals for their help during the preparation of this chapter: Ian Cartwright, Duncan Cragg, Martin Fowler, Robin Shorrock, and Joe Walnes

consumers at the same rate as the service provider because service consumers often couple themselves to the provider by naively expressing the whole of a document schema within their internal logic. Adding schema extension points and performing "just enough" validation of received messages are two well-understood strategies for mitigating the coupling issues.

Services often end up tightly coupled to one another because of the provider-centric basis of the service contract. *Provider contracts* are by their very nature oblivious to the expectations and demands of individual consumers. To remedy this, I suggest orienting service provision around consumer demands, or *consumer contracts*, which express the reasonable expectations a consumer has for the business functionality represented by the service.

A service that imports consumer contracts, and adheres to them whilst exchanging messages with consumers, implements a derived form of provider contract called a *consumer-driven contract*. Drawing on the assertion-based language described elsewhere in this essay, consumer-driven contracts imbue providers with insight into their consumer obligations and focus service evolution around the delivery of the key business functionality demanded by consumers.

The consumer-driven contract pattern is targeted primarily at service communities in which consumers can be identified and influenced, that is, services within the boundaries of an enterprise. There are obvious limitations to the pattern, not least of which are the lack of tool support, its impact on the message-processing pipeline, and the increased complexity and protocol dependence it introduces into a service community. But we believe that when the pattern is applied in the appropriate context, the benefits far outweigh the drawbacks. Despite it seemingly complicating the communications between services, the pattern is decidedly agile insofar as it seeks to promote the kinds of fine-grained insight and rapid feedback upon which organizational agility depends. Some degree of coupling between services is both inevitable and desirable: consumer-driven contracts help make such couplings known, quantifiable, and amenable to analysis. Moreover, the pattern bridges the development, deployment, and operations parts of the system life cycle, allowing us to establish lightweight versioning strategies and anticipate the effects and costs of evolving services, and as such it contributes to fulfilling our duty of care with respect to the total cost of ownership of a system.

9.1 Evolving a Service: An Example

To illustrate some of the problems you might encounter while evolving services, consider a simple Product service that allows consumer applications to search a product catalog.

An example search result document looks like this:

```
<?xml version="1.0" encoding="utf-8"?>
<Products xmlns="urn:example.com:productsearch:products">
  <Product>
        <CatalogueID>101</CatalogueID>
        <Name>Widget</Name>
        <Price>10.99</Price>
        <Manufacturer>Company A</Manufacturer>
        <InStock>Yes</InStock>
  </Product>
  <Product>
        <CatalogueID>300</CatalogueID>
        <Name>Fooble</Name>
        <Price>2.00</Price>
        <Manufacturer>Company B</Manufacturer>
        <InStock>No</InStock>
  </Product>
</Products>
```

The Product service is currently consumed by two applications: an internal marketing application and an external reseller's web application. Both consumers use XSD validation to validate received documents prior to processing them. The internal application uses the CatalogueID, Name, Price, and Manufacturer fields; the external application uses the CatalogueID, Name, and Price fields. Neither uses the InStock field. Though considered for the marketing application, InStock was dropped early in the development life cycle.

One of the most common ways in which you might evolve a service is to add a field to a document on behalf of one or more consumers. But depending on how the provider and consumers have been implemented, even a simple change like this can have costly implications for the business and its partners.

In this example, after the Product service has been in production for some time, a second reseller considers using it but asks that a Description field be added to each product. Because of the way the consumers have been built, the change has significant and costly implications both for the provider and for the existing consumers—the cost to each varying based on how you implement the change. There are at least two ways in which you can distribute the cost of change between the members of the service community. First, you can modify the original schema and require each consumer to update its copy of the schema in order to correctly validate search results; the cost of changing the system is distributed between the provider—who, faced with a change request like this, will always have to make some kind of change—and the existing consumers, who have no interest in the updated functionality. Alternatively, you can choose to expose a second operation and schema to the new consumer and maintain the original operation and schema on behalf of the existing consumers. The cost of change is now constrained to the provider but at the expense of making the service more complex and more costly to maintain.

Even a simple example such as this illustrates the point that once service providers and consumers are in production, providers rapidly find themselves adopting a cautious approach to changing any element of the contract they offer their consumers; this is because they cannot anticipate or gain insight into the ways in which consumers realize their contracts. Without introspecting the function and role of the contracts you implement in your SOA, you subject your services to a form of "hidden" coupling that anyone is rarely equipped to address in any systematic fashion. The absence of programmatic insights into the ways in which a community of services has adopted a contract and the lack of constraints on the contract-driven implementation choices made by service providers and consumers combine to undermine the purported benefits of SOA enabling the enterprise. In short, you burden the enterprise with services.

9.2 Schema Versioning

We'll begin the investigation into the contract and coupling problems that bedevil the example Product service by looking at the issue of schema versioning. The WC3 Technical Architecture Group (TAG) has described a number of versioning strategies that can help you evolve your service's message schemas in ways that mitigate your coupling problems.[2]

Both extremes bring with them problems that inhibit the delivery of business value and exacerbate the total cost of ownership of the

---

2. Proposed TAG Finding, "Versioning XML Languages [editorial draft]," November 16, 2003; http://www.w3.org/2001/tag/doc/versioning.

system. Explicit and implicit "no versioning" strategies result in systems that are alike in being unpredictable in their interactions, being fragile, and being costly to change downstream.

Big bang strategies, on the other hand, give rise to tightly coupled service landscapes where schema changes ripple through providers and consumers, disrupting uptime, retarding evolution, and reducing revenue generating opportunities.

The example service community effectively implements a big bang strategy. Given the costs associated with enhancing the business value of the system, it is clear that the providers and consumers would benefit from a more flexible versioning strategy—what the TAG finding calls a *compatible* strategy—that provides for backward- and forward-compatible schemas. In the context of evolving services, backward-compatible schemas enable consumers of newer schemas to accept instances of an older schema; a service provider built to handle new versions of a backward-compatible request, say, would nonetheless still accept a request formatted according to an old schema. Forward-compatible schemas, on the other hand, enable consumers of older schemas to process an instance of a newer schema. This is the sticking point for the existing Product consumers: if the search result schema had been made forward-compatible when first put into production, the consumers would be able to handle instances of the new version of the search result without breaking or requiring modification.

Extension Points

Making schemas both backward- and forward-compatible is a well-understood design task best expressed by the Must Ignore pattern of extensibility.[3] The Must Ignore pattern recommends that schemas incorporate extensibility points. These extensibility points allow us to add extension elements to types and additional attributes to each element. The pattern also recommends that XML languages define a processing model that specifies how consumers process extensions. The simplest model requires consumers to ignore elements they do not recognize, which is where the pattern gets its name. The model may also require consumers to process elements that have a "Must Understand" flag, or abort if they cannot understand them.

---

3. David Orchard, "Extensibility, XML Vocabularies, and XML Schema"; http://www.pacificspirit.com/Authoring/Compatibility/ExtendingAndVersioningXMLLanguages.html.

This is the schema on which we originally based our search results documents:

```
<?xml version="1.0" encoding="utf-8"?>
<xs:schema xmlns="urn:example.com:productsearch:products"
        xmlns:xs="http://www.w3.org/2001/XMLSchema"
        elementFormDefault="qualified"
        targetNamespace="urn:example.com:productsearch:products"
        id="Products">
  <xs:element name="Products" type="Products" />
  <xs:complexType name="Products">
      <xs:sequence>
        <xs:element minOccurs="0" maxOccurs="unbounded"
                        name="Product" type="Product" />
      </xs:sequence>
  </xs:complexType>
  <xs:complexType name="Product">
      <xs:sequence>
        <xs:element name="CatalogueID" type="xs:int" />
        <xs:element name="Name" type="xs:string" />
        <xs:element name="Price" type="xs:double" />
        <xs:element name="Manufacturer" type="xs:string" />
        <xs:element name="InStock" type="xs:string" />
      </xs:sequence>
  </xs:complexType>
</xs:schema>
```

Let's roll back time to specify a forward-compatible, extensible schema:

```
<?xml version="1.0" encoding="utf-8"?>
<xs:schema xmlns="urn:example.com:productsearch:products"
        xmlns:xs="http://www.w3.org/2001/XMLSchema"
        elementFormDefault="qualified"
        targetNamespace="urn:example.com:productsearch:products"
        id="Products">
  <xs:element name="Products" type="Products" />
  <xs:complexType name="Products">
      <xs:sequence>
        <xs:element minOccurs="0" maxOccurs="unbounded"
                        name="Product" type="Product" />
      </xs:sequence>
  </xs:complexType>
  <xs:complexType name="Product">
      <xs:sequence>
        <xs:element name="CatalogueID" type="xs:int" />
        <xs:element name="Name" type="xs:string" />
        <xs:element name="Price" type="xs:double" />
        <xs:element name="Manufacturer" type="xs:string" />
        <xs:element name="InStock" type="xs:string" />
        <xs:element minOccurs="0" maxOccurs="1"
                        name="Extension" type="Extension" />
      </xs:sequence>
```

```
    </xs:complexType>
    <xs:complexType name="Extension">
        <xs:sequence>
          <xs:any minOccurs="1" maxOccurs="unbounded"
                    namespace="##targetNamespace" processContents="lax" />
        </xs:sequence>
    </xs:complexType>
</xs:schema>
```

This schema includes an optional Extension element at the foot of each product. The Extension element itself can contain one or more elements from the target namespace.

Now when you get a request to add a description to each product, you can publish a new schema containing an additional *Description* element that the provider inserts into the extension container. This allows the Product service to return results that include product descriptions and consumers using the new schema to validate the entire document.

Consumers using the old schema will not break, even though they will not process the description. The new results document looks like this:

```
<?xml version="1.0" encoding="utf-8"?>
<Products xmlns="urn:example.com:productsearch:products">
  <Product>
        <CatalogueID>101</CatalogueID>
        <Name>Widget</Name>
        <Price>10.99</Price>
        <Manufacturer>Company A</Manufacturer>
        <InStock>Yes</InStock>
        <Extension>
          <Description>Our top of the range widget</Description>
        </Extension>
  </Product>
  <Product>
        <CatalogueID>300</CatalogueID>
        <Name>Fooble</Name>
        <Price>2.00</Price>
        <Manufacturer>Company B</Manufacturer>
        <InStock>No</InStock>
        <Extension>
          <Description>Our bargain fooble</Description>
        </Extension>
  </Product>
</Products>
```

The revised schema looks like this:

```
<?xml version="1.0" encoding="utf-8"?>
<xs:schema xmlns="urn:example.com:productsearch:products"
        xmlns:xs="http://www.w3.org/2001/XMLSchema"
        elementFormDefault="qualified"
        targetNamespace="urn:example.com:productsearch:products"
        id="Products">
  <xs:element name="Products" type="Products" />
  <xs:complexType name="Products">
      <xs:sequence>
        <xs:element minOccurs="0" maxOccurs="unbounded"
                        name="Product" type="Product" />
      </xs:sequence>
  </xs:complexType>
  <xs:complexType name="Product">
      <xs:sequence>
        <xs:element name="CatalogueID" type="xs:int" />
        <xs:element name="Name" type="xs:string" />
        <xs:element name="Price" type="xs:double" />
        <xs:element name="Manufacturer" type="xs:string" />
        <xs:element name="InStock" type="xs:string" />
        <xs:element minOccurs="0" maxOccurs="1"
                        name="Extension" type="Extension" />
      </xs:sequence>
  </xs:complexType>
  <xs:complexType name="Extension">
      <xs:sequence>
        <xs:any minOccurs="1" maxOccurs="unbounded"
                    namespace="##targetNamespace"
                    processContents="lax" />
      </xs:sequence>
  </xs:complexType>
  <code:bold><xs:element name="Description"
                        type="xs:string" /></code:bold>
</xs:schema>
```

Note that the first version of the extensible schema is forward-compatible with the second and that the second is backward-compatible with the first. This flexibility, however, comes at the expense of increased complexity. Extensible schemas allow you to make unforeseen changes to an XML language; but by the same token, they provide for requirements that may very well never arise. In so doing, they obscure the expressive power that comes from a simple design and frustrate the meaningful representation of business information by introducing metainformational container elements into the domain language.

I won't discuss schema extensibility further here. Suffice to say, extension points allow you to make backward- and forward-compatible changes to schemas and documents without breaking service providers and consumers. Schema extensions do not, however, help you when you need to make what is ostensibly a breaking change to a contract.

9.3 Breaking Changes

As a value-add, the Product service includes in the search results a field indicating whether the product is currently in stock. The service populates this field using an expensive call into a legacy inventory system—a dependency that's costly to maintain. The service provider wants to remove this dependency, clean up the design, and improve the overall performance of the system—preferably without imposing any of the cost of change on the consumers. Fortunately, none of the consumer applications actually does anything with this value; though expensive, it is redundant.

That's the good news. The bad news is that with our existing setup, if we remove a required component—in this case, the InStock field—from our extensible schema, we will break existing consumers. To fix the provider, we have to fix the entire system. When we remove the functionality from the provider and publish a new contract, each consumer application will have to be redeployed with the new schema. We'll also have to test the interactions between services thoroughly. The Product service in this respect cannot evolve independently of its consumers: provider and consumers must all jump at the same time.

The service community in this example is frustrated in its evolution because each consumer implements a form of "hidden" coupling that naively reflects the entirety of the provider contract in the consumer's internal logic. The consumers, through their use of XSD validation and static language bindings derived from a document schema, implicitly accept the whole of the provider contract, irrespective of their appetite for processing the component parts.

David Orchard provides some clues as to how you might avoid this issue when he alludes to the Internet Protocol's Robustness Principle: "In general, an implementation must be conservative in its sending behavior and liberal in its receiving behavior."

In the context of service evolution, we can augment this principle by saying that message receivers should implement "just enough" validation; that is, they should process only that data that contributes to the business functions they implement and should validate received data only in a bounded or targeted fashion, as opposed to the implicitly unbounded, "all-or-nothing" validation inherent in XSD processing.

Schematron

One way you can improve consumer-side validation is by asserting pattern expressions along the received message's document tree axes, perhaps using a structural tree pattern validation language such as Schematron.[4] Using Schematron, each consumer of the Product service can programmatically assert what it expects to find in the search results:

```
<?xml version="1.0" encoding="utf-8" ?>
<schema xmlns="http://www.ascc.net/xml/schematron">

  <title>ProductSearch</title>
  <ns uri="urn:example.com:productsearch:products" prefix="p"/>

  <pattern name="Validate search results">
      <rule context="*//p:Product">
        <assert test="p:CatalogueID">Must contain
                                   CatalogueID node</assert>
        <assert test="p:Name">Must contain Name node</assert>
        <assert test="p:Price">Must contain Price node</assert>
      </rule>
  </pattern>

</schema>
```

Schematron implementations typically transform a Schematron schema such as this into an XSLT transformation that the message receiver can apply to a document to determine its validity.

Notice that this sample Schematron schema makes no assertions about elements for which the consuming application has no appetite. In this way, the validation language explicitly targets a bounded set of required elements. Changes to the underlying document's schema will not be picked up by the validation process unless they disturb the explicit expectations described in the Schematron schema, even if those changes extend to removing formerly mandatory elements.

Here then is a relatively lightweight solution to the contract and coupling problems: one that doesn't require you to add obscure metainformational elements to a document. So, let's roll back time once again and reinstate the simple schema described at the outset of the chapter. But this time round, we'll insist that consumers are liberal in their receiving behavior. This means they should validate and process only

---

4. Dare Obasanjo, "Designing Extensible, Versionable XML Formats"; http://msdn. microsoft.com/library/en-us/dnexxml/html/xml07212004.asp.

the information that supports the business functions they implement (using Schematron schemas rather than XSD to validate received messages). Now when the provider is asked to add a description to each product, the service can publish a revised schema without disturbing existing consumers. Similarly, on discovering that the InStock field is not validated or processed by any of the consumers, the service can revise the search results schema, again without disturbing the rate of evolution of each consumer.

At the end of this process, the Product results schema looks like this:

```
<?xml version="1.0" encoding="utf-8"?>
<xs:schema xmlns="urn:example.com:productsearch:products"
           xmlns:xs="http://www.w3.org/2001/XMLSchema"
           elementFormDefault="qualified"
           targetNamespace="urn:example.com:productsearch:products"
           id="Products">
  <xs:element name="Products" type="Products" />
  <xs:complexType name="Products">
      <xs:sequence>
        <xs:element minOccurs="0" maxOccurs="unbounded"
                        name="Product" type="Product" />
      </xs:sequence>
  </xs:complexType>
  <xs:complexType name="Product">
      <xs:sequence>
        <xs:element name="CatalogueID" type="xs:int" />
        <xs:element name="Name" type="xs:string" />
        <xs:element name="Price" type="xs:double" />
        <xs:element name="Manufacturer" type="xs:string" />
        <xs:element name="Description" type="xs:string" />
      </xs:sequence>
  </xs:complexType>
</xs:schema>
```

9.4 Consumer-Driven Contracts

The use of Schematron in the previous example leads to some interesting observations about contracts between providers and consumers, with implications beyond document validation. This section generalizes some of these insights and expresses them in terms of a Consumer-Driven Contract pattern.

The first thing to note is that document schemas are only a portion of what a service provider has to offer consumers. You call the sum total of a service's externalized exploitation points the *provider contract*.

Provider Contracts

A provider contract expresses a service provider's business function capabilities in terms of the set of exportable elements necessary to support that functionality. From a service evolution point of view, a contract is a container for a set of exportable business function elements. A non-normative list of these elements includes the following:

- *Document schemas*: We've already discussed document schemas in some detail. Next to interfaces, document schemas are the parts of a provider contract most likely to change as the service evolves; but perhaps because of this, they're also the parts we have most experience of imbuing with service evolution strategies such as extension points and document tree path assertions.

- *Interfaces*: In their simplest form, service provider interfaces comprise the set of exportable operation signatures a consumer can exploit to drive the behavior of a provider. Message-oriented systems typically export relatively simple operation signatures and push the business intelligence into the messages they exchange. In a message-oriented system, received messages drive endpoint behavior according to semantics encoded in the message header or payload. RPC-like services, on the other hand, encode more of their business semantics in their operation signatures. Either way, consumers depend on some portion of a provider's interface to realize business value, so we must account for interface consumption when evolving our service landscape.

- *Conversations*: Service providers and consumers exchange messages in conversations that compose one or more message exchange patterns. Over the course of a conversation, a consumer can expect the messages the provider sends and receives to externalize some state particular to the interaction. For example, a hotel reservation service might offer consumers the ability to reserve a room at the outset of a conversation and to confirm the booking and make a deposit in subsequent message exchanges. The consumer here might reasonably expect the service to "remember" the details of the reservation when engaging in these follow-on exchanges, rather than demand that the parties repeat the entire conversation at each step in the process. As a service evolves, the set of conversational gambits available to provider and consumer might change. Conversations are thus candidates for being considered part of a provider contract.

- *Policy*: Besides exporting document schemas, interfaces, and conversations, service providers may declare and enforce specific usage requirements that govern how the other elements of the contract can be used. Most commonly, these requirements relate to the security and transactional contexts in which a consumer can exploit a provider's functionality. The web services stack typically expresses this policy framework using the WS-Policy generic model plus additional domain-specific policy languages such as WS-SecurityPolicy, but in the context of our considering policies as candidates for being included in a provider contract, our definition of policy is specification and implementation agnostic.[5]

- *Quality of service characteristics*: The business value potential that service providers and consumers exploit is often evaluated in the context of a specific quality of service characteristics such as availability, latency, and throughput. You should consider these characteristics as likely constituents of a provider contract and account for them in your service evolution strategies.

The definition of a contract here is a little broader than the one you might usually hear when talking about services, but from a service evolution perspective it usefully abstracts the significant forces that impact the problem domain. That said, the definition is not meant to be exhaustive in terms of the kinds of elements a provider contract might contain; it refers simply to a logical set of exportable business function elements that are candidates for including in a service evolution strategy. From a logical point of view, this set of candidate elements is open, but in practice, internal or external factors, such as interoperability requirements or platform limitations, may constrain the type of elements a contract can contain. For example, a contract belonging to a service that conforms to the WS-Basic profile will likely not contain policy elements.

Notwithstanding any such constraints, the scope of a contract is determined simply by the cohesion of its member elements. A contract can contain many elements and be broad in scope, or focus narrowly on only a few, so long as it expresses some business function capability.

How do you decide whether to include a candidate contractual element in your provider contract? You ask whether any of your consumers

---

5. "Schematron: A Language for Making Assertions About Patterns Found in XML Documents"; http://www.schematron.com.

might reasonably expect the element's business function capability to continue to be satisfied throughout the service's lifetime. You've already seen how consumers of the example service can express an interest in parts of the document schema exported by the service and how they might assert that their expectations regarding this contractual element continue to be met. Thus, the document schema is part of the provider contract.

Provider contracts have the following characteristics:

- *Closed and complete*: Provider contracts express a service's business function capabilities in terms of the complete set of exportable elements available to consumers and as such are closed and complete with respect to the functionality available to the system.

- *Singular and authoritative*: Provider contracts are singular and authoritative in their expression of the business functionality available to the system.

- *Bounded stability and immutability*: A provider contract is stable and immutable for a bounded period and/or locale.[6] Provider contracts typically use some form of versioning to differentiate differently bounded instances of the contract.

Consumer Contracts

If you decide to account for consumer expectations regarding the schemas you expose—and consider it worth your provider knowing about them—then you need to import those consumer expectations into the provider. The Schematron assertions in this example look very much like the kinds of tests that, given to the provider, might help ensure the provider continues to meet its commitments to its clients. By implementing these tests, the provider gains a better understanding of how it can evolve message structures without breaking the service community. And where a proposed change would in fact break one or more consumers, the provider will have immediate insight into the issue and so be better able to address it with the parties concerned, accommodating their requirements or providing incentives for them to change as business factors dictate.

---

6. WS-Policy; http://www-128.ibm.com/developerworks/library/specification/ws-polfram.

In this example, you can say that the set of assertions generated by all consumers expresses the mandatory structure of the messages to be exchanged during the period in which the assertions remain valid for their parent applications. If the provider were given this set of assertions, it would be able to ensure that every message it sends is valid for every consumer—but only insofar as the set of assertions is valid and complete.

Generalizing this structure, you can distinguish the *provider contract* from the individual contractual obligations that are particular to an instance of a provider-consumer relationship, which I will now call *consumer contracts*. When a provider accepts and adopts the reasonable expectations expressed by a consumer, it enters into a consumer contract.

Consumer contracts have the following characteristics:

- *Open and incomplete*: Consumer contracts are open and incomplete with respect to the business functionality available to the system. They express a subset of the system's business function capabilities from the point of view of a consumer's expectations of the provider contract.

- *Multiple and nonauthoritative*: Consumer contracts are multiple in proportion to the number of consumers of a service. Moreover, each consumer contract is nonauthoritative with regard to the total set of contractual obligations placed on the provider. The nonauthoritative nature of the relationship extending from consumer to provider is one of the key features that distinguishes a service-oriented architecture from a distributed application architecture. Service consumers must recognize that their peers in a service community are liable to consume the provider in ways quite different from their own. Peers may evolve at different rates and demand changes of the provider that potentially disturb the dependencies and expectations residing in other parts of the system. A consumer cannot anticipate how or when a peer will disturb the provider contract; a client in a distributed application has no such concerns.

- *Bounded stability and immutability*: Like provider contracts, consumer contracts are valid for a particular period of time and/or location.

Consumer-Driven Contracts

Consumer contracts allow you to reflect on the business value being exploited at any point in a provider's lifetime. By expressing and asserting expectations of a provider contract, consumer contracts effectively define which parts of that provider contract currently support the business value realized by the system and which do not. This leads me to suggest that service communities might benefit from being specified in the first instance in terms of consumer contracts. In this view, provider contracts emerge to meet consumer expectations and demands. To reflect the derived nature of this new contractual arrangement, you can call such provider contracts *consumer-driven contracts* or *derived contracts*.

The derivative nature of consumer-driven provider contracts adds a heteronomous aspect to the relationship between service provider and consumer. That is, providers are subject to an obligation that originates from outside their boundaries. This in no way impacts the fundamentally autonomous nature of their implementations; it simply makes explicit the fact that for success services depend on their being consumed. *Consumer-driven contracts* have the following characteristics:

- *Closed and complete*: A consumer-driven contract is closed and complete with respect to the entire set of functionality demanded by existing consumers. The contract represents the mandatory set of exportable elements required to support consumer expectations during the period in which those expectations remain valid for their parent applications.
- *Singular and nonauthoritative*: Consumer-driven contracts are singular in their expression of the business functionality available to the system but nonauthoritative because they're derived from the union of existing consumer expectations.
- *Bounded stability and immutability*: A consumer-driven contract is stable and immutable with respect to a particular set of consumer contracts. That is to say, you can determine the validity of a consumer-driven contract according to a specified set of consumer contracts, effectively bounding the forward- and backward-compatible nature of the contract in time and space. The compatibility of a contract remains stable and immutable for a particular set of consumer contracts and expectations but is subject to change as expectations come and go.

Summary of Contract Characteristics

The following table summarizes the characteristics of the three types of contract described in this chapter:

Contract	Open	Complete	Number	Authority	Bounded
Provider	Closed	Complete	Single	Authoritative	Space/time
Consumer	Open	Incomplete	Multiple	Nonauthoritative	Space/time
Consumer-driven	Closed	Complete	Single	Nonauthoritative	Consumers

Implementation

The Consumer-Driven Contract pattern recommends building service communities using consumer and consumer-driven contracts. The pattern does not, however, specify the form or structure consumer and consumer-driven contracts should adopt, and it does not determine how consumer expectations are communicated to the provider and asserted during the provider's lifetime.

Contracts may be expressed and structured in several ways. In their simplest form, consumer expectations can be captured in a spreadsheet or similar document and implemented during the design, development, and testing phases of a provider application. By going a little further and introducing unit tests that assert each expectation, you can ensure that contracts are described and enforced in a repeatable, automated fashion with each build. In more sophisticated implementations, expectations can be expressed as Schematron- or WS-Policy-like assertions that are evaluated at runtime in the input and output pipelines of a service endpoint.

As is the case with the structure of contracts, you have several options when it comes to communicating expectations between providers and consumers. Since the Consumer-Driven Contract pattern is implementation-agnostic, you could, given the appropriate organizational setup, transmit expectations simply by talking to other teams or using email. Where the number of expectations and/or consumers grows too large to manage in this manner, you can consider introducing a contract service interface and implementation into the service infrastructure. Whatever the mechanism, it is likely communications will be conducted out-of-band and prior to any conversations that exercise the business functionality of the system.

Benefits

Consumer-driven contracts offer two significant benefits when it comes to evolving services. First, they focus the specification and delivery of service functionality on key business-value drivers. A service is of value to the business only to the extent it is consumed. Consumer-driven contracts tie service evolution to business value by asserting the value of exportable service community elements, that is, the things consumers require of providers to do their job. As a result, providers expose a lean contract clearly aligned with the business goals that underpin their consumers. Service evolution emerges where consumers express a clear business need by modifying their expectations of the provider.

Of course, your ability to start with a minimal set of requirements and evolve your service to meet changes in consumer expectations presupposes that you are in a position to evolve and operate the service in a controlled and efficient manner. Because they do not capture any of the expectations around service consumption, provider contracts must be supplemented with some other mechanism for monitoring and assessing the impact of change. Consumer contracts, on the other hand, imbue providers with a repository of knowledge and a feedback mechanism that you can draw on during the operations part of the system life cycle. Using the fine-grained insight and rapid feedback you derive from consumer-driven contracts, you can plan changes and assess their impact on applications currently in production. In practice, this allows you to target individual consumers and provide incentives for them to relinquish an expectation that is stopping you from making a change that is not currently backward- and/or forward-compatible.

Consumer-Driven Contracts and SLAs

We've discussed ways in which consumer and consumer-driven contracts express business value. But I should make clear that despite some superficial resemblances to specifications such as WS-Agreement and Web Service Level Agreement (WSLA), consumer-driven contracts are not intended to express service-level agreements.[7] WS-Agreement and WSLA are motivated by the need to provide assurances to consumers regarding quality of service and resource availability and, in the case of WSLA, by the requirement to provision services and allocate resources dynamically. The underlying assumption behind the consumer-driven contract pattern is that services, by themselves, are of

---

7. See http://www-128.ibm.com/developerworks/webservices/library/specification/ws-secpol.

no value to the business; their value is in being consumed. By specifying services in terms of how they are actually being used by consumers, we aim to deliver organizational agility by exploiting business value in a way that allows for controlled service evolution.

That said, both WS-Agreement and WSLA serve as examples of what an automated contracting protocol and infrastructure might look like. Both specifications describe agreement templates that can be composed with any assertion language for representing and monitoring agreement conditions. Agreements are established through web service interfaces that remain independent of the service proper and are monitored by injecting handlers into the service pipeline.

Liabilities

We have identified the motivation for introducing consumer-driven contracts into the service landscape and have described how the Consumer-Driven Contract pattern addresses the forces that determine service evolution. We will end this essay by discussing the scope of the pattern's applicability, together with some of the issues that may arise while implementing consumer and consumer-driven contracts.

The Consumer-Driven Contract pattern is applicable in the context of either a single enterprise or a closed community of well-known services, or more specifically, an environment in which providers can exert some influence over how consumers establish contracts with them.[8] No matter how lightweight the mechanisms for communicating and representing expectations and obligations, providers and consumers must know about, accept, and adopt a set of channels and conventions. This inevitably adds a layer of complexity and protocol dependence to an already complex service infrastructure. The problem is exacerbated by a lack of tools and execution environment support for describing, implementing, and operating contracts.

I've suggested that systems built around consumer-driven contracts are better able to manage breaking changes to contracts. But I don't mean to suggest that the pattern is a cure-all for the problem of breaking changes; when all is said and done, a breaking change is still a

---

8. See the section "Validity of Data in Bounded Space and Time" in Pat Helland's article, "Data on the Outside vs. Data on the Inside: An Examination of the Impact of Service Oriented Architectures on Data"; http://msdn.microsoft.com/library/default.asp?url=/library/en-us/dnbda/html/dataoutsideinside.asp.

breaking change. I do believe, however, that the pattern provides many insights into what actually constitutes a breaking change. Put simply, a breaking change is anything that fails to satisfy an extant consumer expectation. By helping identify breaking changes, the pattern may serve as the foundation for a service versioning strategy. Moreover, as already discussed, service communities that implement the pattern are better placed to anticipate the effects of service evolution and identify potentially breaking changes before they impact the health of the system. Development and operations teams in particular can more effectively plan their evolutionary strategies—perhaps by deprecating contractual elements for a specific period and simultaneously targeting recalcitrant consumers with incentives to move up to new versions of a contract.

Consumer-driven contracts do not necessarily reduce the coupling between services. Schema extensions and "just enough" validation may help reduce the coupling between service providers and consumers, but even loosely coupled services will nonetheless retain a degree of coupling. Although not contributing directly to lessening the dependencies between services, consumer-driven contracts do excavate and put on display some of those residual "hidden" couplings so that providers and consumers can better negotiate and manage them.

Conclusion

An SOA can enable organizational agility and reduce the cost of change only if its services are capable of evolving independently of one another. Overly coupled services result from the way in which consumers naively implement provider contracts. The Must Ignore pattern of schema extension points and the "just enough" schema validation strategy implemented using Schematron assertions benefit consumers by reducing the coupling between themselves and their providers. Service providers, on the other hand, gain more insight into and feedback on their runtime obligations by deriving their contracts from the set of consumer contracts communicated to them by their consumers. Consumer-driven contracts support service evolution throughout the operational lifetime of a service and more closely align the specification and delivery of service functionality with key business goals.

Chapter 10

Domain Annotations

by Erik Doernenburg, Technology Principal

10.1 Domain-Driven Design Meets Annotations

Over the past decade, many people involved in development projects have come to understand that the real complexity in most applications lies in the actual problem domain the software is dealing with. For this reason, the approach that is known as *domain-driven design* follows these two premises:

- For most software projects, the primary focus should be on the domain and domain logic.

- Complex domain designs should be based on a model.

This means that domain-driven design places an object-oriented model of the domain, expressed in terms of the domain, at the heart of software systems. Data is often stored in a relational database, but the main view of the data is in terms of the domain objects, not in terms of tables and stored procedures. Core domain logic is kept in the domain model, rather than being spread across classes in the user interface and the service layers of the application.

Following domain-driven design produces software systems that have a clear separation between the domain model, which is usually long-lived and comparably stable, and application interface and infrastructure code, which are more short-lived and intertwined with specific technologies such as object-relational mappers or web frameworks. The challenge lies in maintaining this separation to keep both halves of the software system reusable; on one hand, it should be possible to use the domain model in several applications or services or upgrade to a new technology stack, and on the other hand, the infrastructure code should be readily usable for arbitrary domain models. The ultimate goal is, of course, the productization of infrastructure code, commercially or as open source software, so that application developers can concentrate on their problem domain.

Domain-Specific Metadata

Develop applications based on the domain model simply and by leveraging automation. Don't require code changes to either the infrastructure code or the domain model. Naturally, this requires heavy use of reflection and generic types, but at the same time the infrastructure code benefits from any metainformation available about the domain.

Much metadata is present as part of the model's implementation. For example, the fact that the relationship between department and employee is a one-to-many relationship can be inferred from the types used for the relationship in the department and employee classes. Using a collection in the department class to hold the employees tells other code that the relationship is a to-many relationship, and a normal object reference to the department in the employee class makes it specifically a one-to-many relationship. Based on this information, a user interface framework can choose an appropriate widget, such as a listbox for the employees, in an autogenerated screen for the department.

Implicit metadata, which is metadata that is present as a necessary part of the implementation, allows for a great deal of automation; however, most applications can benefit from more, and explicit, metadata. This is especially true in the area of validation. In the previous example, the framework that autogenerates maintenance screens has no way to determine whether a department without any employees is valid. If metadata is added to the employees collection to signify that this is a 1..n relationship, then the framework can prevent users from saving a department that has no employees. This information could be provided by using specific collection classes, but modern development platforms include a better construct for this purpose.

Java Annotations and .NET Attributes

The power of metadata to provide abstractions and reduce coupling did not escape the designers of programming languages, and from its first release, the Microsoft .NET platform and its common language runtime (CLR) provided a mechanism for developers to create and add arbitrary metadata to almost any language element. The CLR uses the term *attribute* for this concept. Attributes are defined like other types and can have data and behavior like classes, but they use a special syntax with square brackets to attach to a language element.

The following example demonstrates an attribute in C#; the attribute is intended to specify and validate the maximum length of a property value:

```
[AttributeUsage(AttributeTargets.Property)]
public class MaxLengthAttribute : Attribute
{
    private int maxLength;

    public MaxLengthAttribute(int maxLength)
    {
        this.maxLength = maxLength;
    }

    public void validate(PropertyInfo property, object obj)
    {
        MethodInfo method   = property.GetGetMethod(false);
        string propertyValue = (string)method.Invoke(obj, new object[0]);
        if(propertyValue.Length > maxLength)
        throw new ValidationException( ... );
    }
}
```

Apart from inheriting from Attribute, the AttributeUsage attribute defined by the CLR is attached to the attribute declaration to signal that the attribute must be used with properties, rather than classes or fields, for example. The implementation actually assumes that the property is of type string, but this constraint cannot be expressed as part of the attribute definition. Using reflection to achieve loose coupling, as shown in the validate method, is quite common for attributes. Note that the validate method must be triggered by application code; the CLR does not provide a mechanism to have the code invoked when the target property is accessed.

The attribute could be used in code as in the following example:

```
[MaxLength(50)]
public string Name
{
    get { return name; }
    set { name = value; }
}
```

A similar construct was added to Java in Java 5. In the Java world, the term *annotation* is used, which describes the concept somewhat better and is less overloaded in the context of software development. For this reason, we will use the term *annotation* in the remainder of this essay to refer to all implementations of this concept.

Java also uses a special syntax, in this case involving the @ character, to attach an annotation to a language element. However, there are several marked differences compared to the .NET version. Java does not use inheritance to define an annotation but uses a new keyword, namely, @interface, for that purpose. It does not specify where an attribute can be used, but it does specify to which stage of the development cycle it should be retained. The most important difference, though, is that Java annotations cannot contain code; they are more like interfaces than classes. This means that where .NET can use constructors to provide default values, Java annotations have to use the special default keyword.

A graver consequence is that the validation behavior must be written in an external class. In itself this is not a disaster, but it does work against the principle of encapsulation. Where the .NET version keeps the max length value private and contains the validation logic, a Java version has to make the value public and has to pass the annotation into the validation method in another class. As a code smell, this is "feature envy," and it results in parallel class hierarchies. It should be noted, though, that most uses of annotations do not lend themselves to contain behavior like this, and therefore most uses of Java annotations and .NET attributes follow the same patterns.

Domain Annotations

A logical name for annotations that are used to express information about the domain is *domain annotations*.

Domain annotations have three distinct characteristics:

- They are added to language elements in domain objects only, that is, to the classes, to domain-specific public methods, or possibly to arguments of such methods.

- They are defined in the domain model in the same package/namespace as the domain objects.

- They provide information that can be used by more than one area of functionality in the application.

The first item in the previous list can be seen as a truly defining characteristic. Annotations on objects not in the domain model are clearly outside the scope of the domain. And although some environments require domain objects to implement specific methods, ranging from the simple case of equal and hash code methods to more complex examples such as serialization, it is highly unlikely that domain annotations will provide value on such methods. Similarly, private methods are obviously internal to an object's implementation, and therefore it should not be necessary to provide additional information about them.

Of course, there are also exceptions to the rule: the one-to-many example in the previous section shows metadata that is useful in many different domains, which is why, for example, the EJB3 standard provides the generic @OneToMany annotation. However, an annotation like this that is not defined in the domain model but in an infrastructure framework contradicts the second rule, and using it couples the domain model to the EJB3 specification. Worse, if other application infrastructure code needs this information as well, it also becomes coupled to the EJB3 specification. There is an obvious conflict between keeping the domain model free of dependencies on infrastructure code and having generic infrastructure code that requires specific annotations to do its magic. As usual, there is no categorical answer to the question of when to use which.

The Case for Domain Annotations

I mentioned before that annotations provide data, and in the case of CLR attribute behavior, they are never part of the execution path of annotated elements. This means that extra code is required to use the annotation. Despite the additional code, annotations can still result in less overall code and a clearer implementation. Consider an alternative approach to the max length validation example. It would be possible to add, by convention or an explicit interface, a validation method to the domain objects. This could contain code like the following Java code:

```java
public void validate()
{
    if(getName().length > 50)
        throw new ValidationException("Name must be 50 characters or less");
    if(getAddressLineOne().length > 60)
        throw new ValidationException(
                        "Address line one must be 60 characters or less");
    /* more validation of the object's state omitted */
}
```

It is obvious that such a method is quite problematic because it mixes several concerns. Imagine, for example, that at a later stage the system has to be capable of reporting multiple problems at the same time. For this reason, most developers would extract a method to report the validation problem, which would leave the code as follows:

```
public void validate()
{
    if(getName().length > 50)
        validationError("Name", 50);
    if(getAddressLineOne().length > 60)
        validationError("AddressLineOne", 60);
    /* more validation of the object's state omitted */
}
```

A further step that increases the level of abstraction is to create a single validation method that retrieves the value and carries out the check. Its implementation would use reflection, and the remaining code in the validate method could look as follows:

```
public void validate()
{
    validate("name", 50);
    validate("addressLineOne", 60);
}
```

In this case, all code that can possibly be abstracted is moved into a single method; all that is left in the validate method is a list of metadata. However, this is arguably better kept in an annotation:

```
@MaxLength(50)
public String getName()
{
    /* implementation omitted */
}
```

Not only does using an annotation keep the length information about the name next to the getName method, but, more important, it also avoids the use of strings to refer to methods. The only additional code needed in comparison to the previous version is a loop over all methods to find the ones that have the MaxLength annotation.

10.2 Case Study: Leroy's Lorries

Rather than being invented by a smart person, design patterns are observed in existing code. The same holds true for domain annotations, and this section presents two domain annotations that are quite similar to the first annotations we used in this way. (This example won't use the

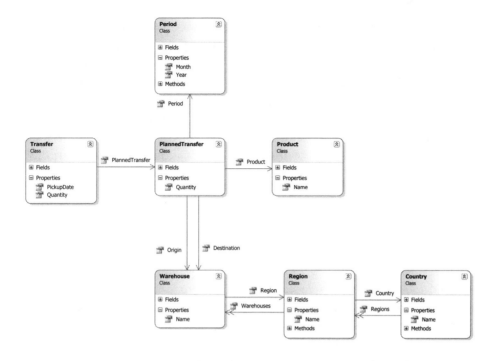

Figure 10.1: TRANSFERS

exact annotations or the original source code for commercial reasons; they were part of a project that ThoughtWorks delivered for a client.)

Leroy's Lorries is a small sample application that my colleague Mike Royle and I prepared to show how to use domain annotations. It is based on our experience from the ThoughtWorks project mentioned earlier, and as in the original project, the problem domains are logistics and shipping. The code is written such that it would work in a smart client application—a Windows application that maintains data on a server but can work in disconnected mode. Like the original application, we used C# as the implementation language, but we upgraded to the newer 2.0 version of the language to make the code clearer.

The Domain Model

For the purpose of this case study, two areas of the domain model are of interest. One is concerned with modeling the transfer of products between warehouses, and the another is concerned with modeling users of the system and their roles.

At the center of the transfer model is the PlannedTransfer domain object, which represents a planned transfer of a certain quantity of product from an origin warehouse to a destination warehouse in a period, which is a month in a given year. An actual transfer that has taken place is represented by the Transfer domain object, which has a reference to the planned transfer to which it corresponds. A transfer also contains the actual pickup date, which does not have to be within the period originally planned, and the quantity of the product that was actually transferred.

Also relevant are a few domain objects concerned with geography. Warehouses, which are the origins and destinations of transfers, are located in regions that in turn are located in countries.

For the purpose of this case study, all the domain objects have been reduced to the properties required to demonstrate how to use the two domain annotations. In the real model that Leroy's Lorries is based on—for example, the product contained seven properties—different types of transfers were modeled by six different classes and had properties such as mode of transport and a reference to the contract. This is important to bear in mind when considering alternative approaches that might seem reasonable for this simplified model.

The user domain object represents users of the system. In this simplified model, users have a name; are associated with a country, which is the country they work in; and can have multiple roles. Possible roles are Planner, Country Admin, and Global Admin. Planners are users who create and modify planned transfers; country administrators maintain warehouse, region, and user data for their countries; and global administrators can set up new countries and designate country administrators.

Data Classification

The first domain annotation concerns itself with classifying data. In the previous description of the domain model, all domain objects were treated in the same way—as objects that describe concepts of the domain. At one point, though, warehouse, region, and country were described as geographical data, which shows that they represent entities that have something in common. Also, in the description of the roles, users can have a distinction between different classes of data that different roles can manipulate.

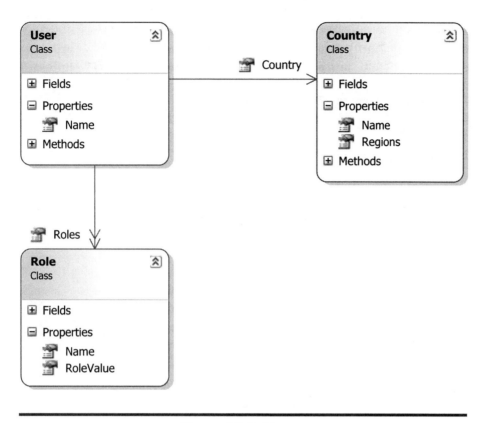

Figure 10.2: USERS

Clearly, the domain has more information about the domain objects than is currently represented, and perhaps unsurprisingly at this point, we use annotations to express this.

The annotation used in Leroy's Lorries is the DataClassification annotation, and it is used to place the domain objects into one of the following four categories:

- *Reference data*: Country, region, warehouse, product, user

- *Transactional data*: Period, transfer, planned transfer

- *Configuration*: Role

- *Audit*: Audit record

The implementation uses an enum to express the categories, and the attribute has no functionality beyond storing the classification for a given class, which means that a Java version would look very similar:

```
namespace LeroysLorries.Model.Attributes
{
    public enum DataClassificationValue
    {
        Reference,
        Transactional,
        Configuration,
        Audit
    }

    [AttributeUsage(AttributeTargets.Class)]
    public class DataClassificationAttribute : Attribute
    {
        private DataClassificationValue classification;

        public DataClassificationAttribute(
                            DataClassificationValue classification)
        {
            this.classification = classification;
        }

        public DataClassificationValue Classification
        {
            get { return classification; }
        }
    }
}
```

The most common query is to get the classification for a given type, and for that reason you can create a small method in a helper class to provide this information in this code:

```
public static DataClassificationValue GetDataClassification(Type classToCheck)
{
    return
        GetAttribute<DataClassificationAttribute>(classToCheck).Classification;
}

private static T GetAttribute<T>(Type classToCheck)
{
    object[] attributes = classToCheck.GetCustomAttributes(typeof(T), true);
    if (attributes.Length == 0)
        throw new ArgumentException( ... );
    return (T)attributes[0];
}
```

The public method would also make sense as a static method on the attribute class itself, thus keeping the entire API in one place. In that case, the generic method should be made public in a helper class so that it can be reused.

Alternatives

There are alternatives to using annotations in order to classify data. An obvious solution is to use inheritance. We could have created a common base class for all reference data, maybe ReferenceDataObject, and make Country, Region, and so on, inherit from it. The same would work for the other classes of domain objects. However, Java and the standard .NET languages do not allow multiple inheritance, which makes inheritance a card that can be played only once, and we felt that we might need inheritance for another problem dimension.

A more theoretical but stronger argument against using inheritance to classify data lies in domain-driven design, which requires shared ownership of the model between the domain experts and the technical people. Inheritance expresses an is-a relationship, and although nobody would have a problem stating that "region is a location," if we chose to create such a parent class for region and country, it simply makes no sense in the real world to say a region is a reference data object. In short, the argument stipulates that the domain object inheritance should be used to model real-world taxonomies and nothing else.

Probably the most straightforward approach to adding classification data to the domain objects is to use an interface with one method:

```
interface DataClassification
{
    DataClassificationValue GetDataClassification();
}
```

All domain objects implement this interface and have hard-coded return values as follows:

```
public DataClassificationValue GetDataClassification()
{
    return DataClassificationValue.Transactional;
}
```

Going down this route requires additional code, and the method on the domain object stands out insofar as the return value is constant for every instance; it is metadata and not data.

A static method would suit the problem better; however, in Java and C#, interfaces cannot contain static methods, and polymorphism is also impossible on static methods.

Another solution to classify data is to use marker interfaces, that is, interfaces without methods. This is a possible workaround in languages that do not have annotations, but it means using a language element that was designed for one purpose, namely, to declare methods for polymorphic references, for something else, and for storing metadata.

Furthermore, if we had used interfaces in such a way, it is likely that we would have created a base interface, DataClassification, for example, and four subinterfaces corresponding to the possible classification values. This would have made it possible to ask an object whether it is ReferenceData but also whether it is DataClassification, somehow mixing up the classification of a domain object and the storage of the classification data.

Use in Auditor

The first use of the DataClassification annotation occurred in the audit logic to implement the following business rule:

- Audit records should be created only for reference data changes.

This rule is implemented in the Auditor class, which is responsible for creating the actual audit records. It uses the helper method described earlier.

```
private bool ShouldAudit(Type type)
{
    DataClassificationValue classification =
        ReflectionHelper.GetDataClassification(type);
    return classification == DataClassificationValue.Reference;
}
```

The information needed to decide whether to create an audit record is stored as an annotation in the domain object, but the logic acting on this information is in the Auditor class. Usually, it is beneficial to keep data and behavior together, but in this case, a case for a domain annotation, the same data will be used for multiple purposes, which means the only way to keep data and behavior together would be to keep all behavior related to this annotation in one place. The next sections show that the uses of this annotation are quite different, which makes separating them a good idea.

Use in PermissionChecker

The following business rule is also implemented using the same Data-Classification annotation:

- Only global administrators can modify all reference data.

Using the same reflection helper method, the implementation of a method in the PermissionChecker class, which decides whether an object can be changed, is extremely simple and focused on the implementation of the business logic:

```
public bool CanChangeObject(User user, object anObject)
{
    DataClassificationValue classification =
        ReflectionHelper.GetDataClassification(anObject.GetType());
    switch(classification)
    {
        case DataClassificationValue.Reference:
            return user.HasRole(RoleValue.GlobalAdmin)
        default:
            return true;
    }
}
```

The difference from the previous code is that the decision is not based directly on the value of the annotation, but the value is used to select a rule appropriate for the classification.

Use in Loader

As mentioned in the introduction, Leroy's Lorries is a smart client application that can work disconnected from the server. This means a working set of data must be downloaded to the client before going offline, and this set should be as small as possible to minimize server load and download volume.

In this context, the data classification is used to implement the following rule:

- Transactional data should be loaded only for planners.

The implementation is almost identical to the previous one but highlights an advantage of using annotations over concrete methods on the domain objects. We pass in the type of the object because when this method is invoked, no instances exist; this method decides whether to create objects.

```
private bool ShouldLoad(Type type, User user)
{
    DataClassificationValue classification =
        ReflectionHelper.GetDataClassification(type);
    if(classification == DataClassificationValue.Transactional)
        return user.HasRole(RoleValue.Planner);
    return true;
}
```

The original application that Leroy's Lorries is based on had more complex rules with more cases that made the use of annotations for data classification even more compelling than shown here.

Navigational Hints

The second domain annotation I'll present in this essay is related to indirect relationships in the domain model. For example, even though Warehouse has no direct relationship with Country, it is possible to say which country a warehouse is located in because of the relationships from warehouse to region and from region to country. Indirect relationships are obviously not confined to objects with the same classification, regional in this case. Looking at the domain model, a transfer, for example, is also related to a country; actually, two countries as planned transfers have relationships to two warehouses.

In Leroy's Lorries, we chose annotations to mark those properties that need to be followed to eventually arrive at a target object, a country, for example. Following properties means retrieving the related domain object and then searching for a property with the same annotation on the resulting object to continue the search.

The implementation of the annotation is even simpler than that of the classification because no value is needed. This again implies that a Java version would be very similar:

```
namespace LeroysLorries.Model.Attributes
{
    [AttributeUsage(AttributeTargets.Property)]
    public class CountrySpecificationAttribute : Attribute
    {
    }
}
```

The attribute used on the properties for the relationships, as well as the Warehouse class from Leroy's Lorries minus any code that pertains to the name of the warehouse, looks like the code on the next page.

```
namespace LeroysLorries.Model.Entities
{
    [DataClassification(DataClassificationValue.Reference)]
    public class Warehouse
    {
        private Region region;

        [CountrySpecification]
        public Region Region
        {
            get { return region; }
            set { region = value; }
        }
    }
}
```

Complementing the annotation is a generic pathfinder class that allows you to get a target object as well as an array of strings describing the path followed from a given type to the target. The following two examples illustrate its use:

```
Warehouse warehouse; // get this from somewhere
PathFinder<Country> finder = new PathFinder<Country>();
Country country = finder.GetTargetObject(warehouse);
```

After creating a pathfinder that targets countries, the pathfinder is used to get the country for a given warehouse. It is noteworthy that the pathfinder uses a convention to determine which attribute to follow.

It simply appends SpecificationAttribute to the type name, Country in this case, and then looks for an attribute with that name in the Attributes namespace. The reason for creating a generic pathfinder will become obvious later in this essay.

```
PathFinder<Country> finder = new PathFinder<Country>();
string[] path = finder.GetPath(typeof(Warehouse));
```

In this second example, the pathfinder returns the path it would have followed as a string array, which contains the strings "Region" and "Country" representing the names of the properties in the Warehouse and Region classes, respectively. This method can obviously be used before any instances of domain objects exist because it works with types, not instances.

```
public class PathFinder<T>
{
    private static string NAMESPACE = "LeroysLorries.Model.Attributes.";
    private Type attrType;
```

```csharp
public PathFinder()
{
    string typeName = NAMESPACE + typeof(T).Name + "SpecificationAttribute";
    if((attrType = Type.GetType(typeName)) == null)
        throw new ArgumentException( ... );
}

public T GetTargetObject(object anObject)
{
    Type objectType = anObject.GetType();
    if(objectType == typeof(T))
        return (T)anObject;
    PropertyInfo propInfo = ReflectionHelper.GetPropertyWithAttribute(
                                          objectType, attrType);
    object nextObject = ReflectionHelper.GetPropertyValue(
                                          anObject, propInfo.Name);
    return GetTargetObject(nextObject);
}

public string[] GetPath(Type type)
{
    List<string> path = new List<string>();
    if(BuildPath(type, path) == false)
        throw new ArgumentException( ... );
    return path.ToArray();
}

private bool BuildPath(Type type, List<string> path)
{
    if(type == typeof(T))
        return true;
    PropertyInfo prop = ReflectionHelper.GetPropertyWithAttribute(
                                          type, attrType);
    if(prop == null)
        return false;
    path.Add(prop.Name);
    return BuildPath(prop.PropertyType, path);
}
}
```

Alternatives

As with the classification example, there are alternatives to using annotations. In this case, the most obvious choice would be to implement a
property for the relevant type on every domain object, hard-coding the
relationship directly.

For example, the following property would be added to warehouse:

```
public Country Country
{
    get { return region.Country; }
}
```

The country pathfinder, rather than searching for a property with the country specification, would now simply invoke the property that is typed as Country. Although this is still nicely encapsulated object-oriented code, it requires a lot of discipline and legwork to maintain on the domain model.

A more automated approach, which does not require additional code on the domain model, would employ graph searching. The domain object types and their relationships can be seen as a directed graph, and starting from a domain object standard depth-first-search or breadth-first, a search algorithm could be used to find the target object. This would work on instances as well as types, thus allowing for a full implementation of the pathfinder.

With some caching of paths that have been discovered by the search algorithm, this approach could work well, at least as long as the paths are unambiguous and do not require domain logic. Unfortunately, in Leroy's Lorries, this is not the case. Planned transfers have an origin and a destination warehouse, and if these are in different countries, a search algorithm requires additional information to choose which one to follow. Using annotations, the country specification is added to the origin property, reflecting the domain knowledge that planned transfers should be listed under the origin country.

Use in PermissionChecker

Returning to the permission checker described earlier, we use the country specification in the implementation of the following business rule:

- Country administrators can change reference data only for their own country.

The implementation extends the CanChangeObject() method. Adding the new rule to the switch case for reference data, it looks like the code shown on the next page.

```
public bool CanChangeObject(User user, object anObject)
{
    DataClassificationValue classification =
        ReflectionHelper.GetDataClassification(anObject.GetType());
    switch(classification)
    {
        case DataClassificationValue.Reference:
            if(user.HasRole(RoleValue.GlobalAdmin))
                return true;
            if(user.HasRole(RoleValue.CountryAdmin))
                return FindCountry(anObject) == user.Country;
            return false;
        default:
            return true;
    }
}
```

Global administrators can still change all reference data, but for country administrators, the country for the reference data domain object must match the administrator's. The actual use of the pathfinder is extracted into a helper method to keep the code clearer:

```
private Country FindCountry(object anObject)
{
    return new PathFinder<Country>().GetTargetObject(anObject);
}
```

This example not only shows different uses of the individual annotations, but it also shows how both work together to provide a clear and concise implementation of the business rule, without sacrificing separation of concerns.

Use in Loader

Planners are assigned to a country and handle the transfers only for that given country. Similarly, country administrators can maintain data only for their country. When considering the data volume that is downloaded to the client application, it is an obvious optimization to trim the data following this rule:

- Only data for the user's country should be loaded, unless they are global admins.

Using the country specifications and a pathfinder, it is possible to determine a path for each domain object class that leads to the country object. It is then up to the object-relational mapping technology to turn this into a query criterion that limits the objects fetched into memory.

The following code shows an abstracted implementation of the idea:

```
private Query CreateQuery(Type type, User user)
{
    QueryBuilder builder = new QueryBuilder(type);
    if(!user.HasRole(RoleValue.GlobalAdmin))
    {
        PathFinder<Country> finder = new PathFinder<Country>();
        string[] path = finder.GetPath(type);
        builder.AppendCondition(path, QueryBuilder.EQUALS, user.Country);
    }
    return builder.GetQuery();
}
```

This method would obviously be called, and the objects loaded, only when the ShouldLoad() method described in the previous section returns true for the type/user combination.

In Leroy's Lorries, geography is only one important dimension. Equally important is time and the planners' work in monthly planning cycles. This means that, except for historical reference, planners are interested in data only for three months: the current, the previous, and the next month. So, rather than loading years worth of data, we implemented the following rule and lazy loading for other data:

- Transactional data should be loaded only for the previous, current, and next month.

This rule is in addition to the rule presented earlier that stipulates transactional data should be loaded only for planners.

With the pathfinder's generic implementation and the convention for naming and finding the specification attributes, we were able to create the following attribute and place it on the domain objects representing transfers and planned transfers:

```
namespace LeroysLorries.Model.Attributes
{
    [AttributeUsage(AttributeTargets.Property)]
    public class PeriodSpecificationAttribute : Attribute
    {
    }
}
```

Following this, we extended the CreateQuery() method described earlier as follows:

```
private Query CreateQuery(Type type, User user)
{
    QueryBuilder builder = new QueryBuilder(type);
    if(!user.HasRole(RoleValue.GlobalAdmin))
    {
        PathFinder<Country> finder = new PathFinder<Country>();
        string[] path = finder.GetPath(type);
        builder.AppendCondition(path, user.Country);
    }
    if(ReflectionHelper.GetDataClassification(type) ==
    DataClassificationValue.Transactional)
    {
        PathFinder<Period> finder = new PathFinder<Period>();
        string[] path = finder.GetPath(type);
        builder.AppendCondition(path, period);
    }
    return builder.GetQuery();
}
```

I believe this final example shows how neatly different concerns are separated by using domain annotations and generic algorithms based on them. An optimization in the data layer that exploits some domain knowledge is clearly split into the domain part, which is implemented in the domain model, and none of the data access logic leaks out of the data layer.

This example also brings together all three annotations from the case study, which shows again that the annotations are used to implement cross-cutting concerns, which are best kept in a separate area of the codebase.

10.3 Summary

Annotations in Java and attributes in C# have added a construct to these programming languages that enables developers to express metadata in a clear and extensible way. When following a domain-driven design process, metadata belonging to the application domain is expressed as annotations on domain objects; we propose the term *domain annotations* for these annotations. They are strictly limited to the domain model, are normally defined in the same package/namespace as the domain model, and are usually useful for multiple purposes.

Using domain annotations makes it easier to separate domain-specific code from infrastructure code, allowing for independent reuse. The benefit of this separation is twofold. All knowledge about the domain is expressed in a domain model that can be reused with different infrastructure technologies, and infrastructure code can be productized, commercially or as open source software. This means that application developers can focus on the application domain and create something of lasting value.

Chapter 11

Refactoring Ant Build Files

by Julian Simpson, Build Architect

11.1 Introduction

A bad software build system seems to actively resist change. The most innocent change can stop your colleagues from being able to work. Such a reputation won't encourage people to try to improve a build if it eventually gets the job done. This essay will show you how to help ease some of that pain and allow change to take place by describing some short refactorings to apply to your Ant build file. Each refactoring is expressed as a "before" and "after" code example (separated by an arrow to show the direction of transformation) with an explanation. You will be left with some concrete tools that you can apply to your Ant build to make it smaller, more legible, and easier to modify.

What Is Refactoring? And What Is Ant?

Refactoring is the art of making small changes to a system to improve the readability, clarity, or ease of maintenance of a codebase. Refactoring doesn't change functionality; it's used to make the internals of a codebase easier to work on.

Ant is the build tool of choice for many Java-based software projects. It was written at a time when XML seemed to be the answer to any problem in software development. Hence, a project's dependencies are described in an XML file, typically called build.xml. This is the Java equivalent of a Makefile. Ant has been very successful as an open source project, but as projects grow, flex, and become more complicated, it generally becomes hard to maintain.

When Should You Refactor? When Should You Run Away?

Before we get into the details of each refactoring, let's set the context and purpose of the whole exercise. Most of us are here to deliver working software. To do that, you need to be able to build it. Sometimes you'll need to change the build. If nobody wants to change the build, you can't deliver. And that's bad.

So, this essay is an attempt to lower the cost (or pain) of that change. Obviously you need to consider the big picture. Is the build a major source of pain? Is it slowing down the rate at which you can deliver software? Are the issues on the project much larger than the build? Should you head for the door right now?

So, you're still here, and your build is still a problem. How big a problem is it? If you have a real spaghetti monster, this essay is for you, but proceed very, very carefully. Start looking at what you can delete. You may have some targets that aren't used. Start with them. I have successfully used the Simian similarity analyzer on projects to find the duplications that hurt so much and then used Extract Macrodef or Extract Target to address them.

Most of these refactorings can coexist. The previous extraction refactorings can be mutually exclusive in some situations—there may be no difference in the effect of either. There is a wide range of motivations for performing them. You may want to make sure that the code is more easily understood by the casual reader (replacing "comment" with "description"), and you may want to stop the build from being used in unintended ways (by enforcing internal targets).

Can You Refactor a build.xml File?

During a refactoring exercise, a build file's external behavior is easy to define. Given some source files, you generally want some artifacts generated—compiled code, test results, documentation, or a deployable artifact like a WAR file.

Ant build files are equally as deserving of refactoring as business code. They are less tolerant of errors than programming languages. Some errors won't break the build immediately but will cause the build to fail in interesting ways later. For example, failing to set a property will not cause the build to exit in the same way that an undeclared variable will in Java, Ruby, or Python. The challenge is to apply refactoring techniques with discipline but without a testing safety net or IDE tools.

Refactoring usually relies heavily on unit tests to ensure that the refactoring has no functional impact on the code. In this case, we don't have many tools to help us see the impact of the change. There is no ubiquitous test framework like Java's JUnit or Ruby's Test::Unit and no convenient way to isolate a unit for testing with stubbed dependencies. Even if you did have these tools, they may be of questionable value. Should you need a build system that is so complex that you need to test-drive it?

To make matters worse, Ant has static typing without the benefit of compile-time class checking, and the build file is expressed as an XML file that can never be validated because there is no fixed DTD. Changes to a poorly factored build file often have a high risk because a single change can impact productivity. At the beginning of the refactoring process, it may be difficult to test your changes locally before checking in. You may need to make very small changes and test frequently. As you simplify the internal structure of the build, you should gain more traction and be able to make more aggressive refactorings.

11.2 Ant Refactoring Catalog

Each refactoring has a name, a brief description, and an example of the refactoring in action. The first code snippet is the original code, and the snippet after the arrow shows the refactored code. A longer explanation follows the snippets, and some refactorings have an extra sidebar.

Refactoring	Description
Extract macrodef.	Take small blocks of Ant code, and pull out into macrodef with appropriate name.
Extract target.	Take part of a large target, declare it as an independent target, and declare as a dependency of the former.
Introduce declaration.	Make targets declare their dependencies.
Replace call with dependency.	Replace invocations of antcall with intertarget dependencies.
Introduce filtersfile.	Use a property file in a filterset rather than nested filter elements.

(cont.)

Refactoring	Description
Introduce property file.	Move properties from the body of your build.xml file to a flat file.
Move target to wrapper build.	Take targets that aren't used by developers to a higher-level file, and invoke the developer build.
Replace a comment with a description.	Annotate elements with the description attribute instead of XML comments.
Push deployment code into import.	Import deployment code from an external build file so you can import the correct file at build time.
Move element to Antlib.	Share frequently used tasks between projects in an Antlib.
Replace large library definitions with a fileset.	Use a fileset to discover your libraries using a glob rather than specifying the path to each one.
Move runtime properties.	Ensure some separation between the properties that you use to build your code and the runtime configuration.
Reuse elements by ID.	Declare an instance of a type once (for example, a fileset), and make references to it elsewhere to avoid duplication.
Move property outside target.	Put properties into the body of the build.xml so they don't give the illusion that they are scoped to the target (they aren't).
Replace value attribute with location.	Represent filesystem paths with the location attribute so that Ant will normalize the path.
Push wrapper script into build.xml file.	Put input validation and classpath manipulation inside the build.xml file in a cross-platform Ant script.
Add taskname attribute.	Show the intent of the task at runtime by adding the taskname attribute.

(cont.)

Refactoring	Description
Enforce internal target.	Disable internal targets from being invoked from the command line.
Move outputs directory to parent.	Keep all outputs from the build under a single tree.
Replace Exec with Apply.	Use pathlike structures as inputs to execution rather than a list of arg elements.
Use CI publishers.	Tag your build and publish artifacts after the developer build has completed, not during the build.
Introduce distinct target naming.	Use a different punctuation for targets and properties to enhance readability.
Rename target with noun.	Name targets with the output of the target, rather than the process that is applied.

Extract Macrodef

Summary: Macrodefs can be used to tease out small parts of a confused build file.

`refactoring_before.xml`

```xml
<target name="build_and_war_foo.war">
    <javac srcdir="src/foo" destdir="classes/foo" />
    <copy todir="${classes.dir}">
        <filterset>
            <filter token="ENV" value="${environment}" />
        </filterset>
        <fileset dir="config" />
    </copy>
    <war destfile="foo.war">
        <fileset dir="${classes.dir}" />
    </war>
    <move todir="archives" file="foo.war" />
</target>
```

```xml
<macrodef name="build_code">
    <attribute name="component" />
    <sequential>
        <javac srcdir="src/@{component}" destdir="classes/@{component}" />
        <copy todir="${classes.dir}">
            <filterset>
                <filter token="ENV" value="${environment}" />
            </filterset>
            <fileset dir="config" />
        </copy>
    </sequential>
</macrodef>

<macrodef name="make_war">
    <attribute name="component" />
    <sequential>
        <war destfile="@{component}.war">
            <fileset dir="${classes.dir}" />
        </war>
        <move todir="archives" file="@{component}.war" />
    </sequential>
</macrodef>

<target name="foo.war" >
    <build_code component="foo"/>
    <make_war component="foo"/>
</target>
```

Large targets in Ant have the same smell as large methods in an OO language. They can be brittle, hard to test, and hard to debug, and they can't easily be reused.

Making changes to them can be hard because each line may have an implicit dependency on others in the target. Long targets can also confuse the reader as to the intent of the build file author.

The macrodef task is a container task (which wraps the sequential or parallel tasks, which themselves contain the tasks you want to reuse) that can be invoked anywhere in your build file, with attributes. The attributes can be defaulted, which is handy when you might have several uses for a particular macrodef.

Macrodefs also lend themselves well to reuse. In the previous example, a target is doing too much, and we can pull out part of the target to isolate bits of XML. We may take the further step of introducing a target.

```
refactoring_before.xml

<target name="bar.war">
 <war warfile="bar.war" basedir="classes/bar"/>
</target>

<target name="baz.war">
 <war warfile="baz.war" basedir="classes/baz"/>
</target>
```

⬇

```
refactoring_after.xml

<macrodef name="war">
 <attribute name="name"/>
   <sequential>
       <war warfile="'@{name}.war" basedir="classes/@{name}"/>
   </sequential>
 </macrodef>
```

Build files can be very prone to duplication. Macrodefs are good replacements for antcall, which was used in older versions of Ant (before Ant 1.6) for reuse. The previous example contains duplication, which you replace with many calls to a single macrodef, passing different attributes.

How far should you go writing macrodefs? By all means, write large macrodefs if you need to do complex things, but make sure you don't introduce macrodefs that might be better expressed as targets. The XML language may prove hard to scale; you may also want to consider writing your own Ant tasks in Java or a dynamic language. You can try to enjoy the best of both worlds by writing your task in a dynamic language such as Ruby or Python using the scriptdef task. You get to write tested code, with no compilation. Be aware that you need to spend some time learning the object model of Ant.

Extract Target

Summary: Break up targets that appear to be doing different kinds of tasks into two or more targets.

```
refactoring_before.xml

<target name="test" >

   <javac srcdir="${test.src}" destdir="${test.classes}">
     <classpath refid="test.classpath"/>
   </javac>
```

```xml
    <junit failureproperty="test.failure">
       <batchtest todir="${test.results}">
                 <fileset dir="${test.results}"
                    includes="**/*Test.class"/>
          </batchtest>
       </junit>
    </target>
```

⬇

`refactoring_after.xml`

```xml
<target name="compile_tests" depends="compile_code">
    <javac srcdir="${test.src}" destdir="${test.classes}">
       <classpath refid="test.classpath"/>
    </javac>
</target>

<target name="unit_tests" depends="compile_tests">
    <junit failureproperty="test.failure">
       <batchtest todir="${test.results}">
          <fileset dir="${test.results}"
                includes="**/*Test.class"/>
       </batchtest>
    </junit>
 </target>
```

Long Ant targets can be hard to understand, troubleshoot, or add to. The easiest short-term change to make is to add things to existing targets, so that's what people do. Teasing the functional parts into separate targets with the correct dependencies helps you keep a build.xml file cleaner and easier to maintain.

When should you extract a macrodef, and when should you extract a target? If you have a block of code that has dependencies, make it a target. If you want to call it from the command line, for example, a target to drop your private database schema, make it a target. In fact, almost all the time you'll want to make targets. If you have something that seems to be a duplicate block of code, perhaps with different paths or inputs, extract a macrodef so you can invoke with a different attribute. Compilation and unit testing in large projects that may have many source trees and many kinds of tests are good candidates to have targets that invoke a macrodef to do the work.

Another useful trick is to call a macrodef when you might otherwise be tempted to use an antcall; a real-world example is an antcall to a target that checked for build status. antcall can also be slow, because internally it needs to create a new project object.

Introduce Declaration

Summary: Use Ant's built-in declarative logic to replace if conditions, which can be hard to debug.

`refactoring_before.xml`

```
<target name="deploy">
    <if>
     <equals arg1="${j2ee.server}" arg2="was" />
     <then>
       <antcall target="was_deploy"/>
     </then>
     <else>
       <antcall target="weblogic_deploy"/>
     </else>
    </if>
</target>
```

⬇

`refactoring_after.xml`

```
<property name="j2ee.server" value="was" />
<import file="${j2ee.server}.build.xml" />
<!-- there is now a an appropriate target named
        deploy depending on the version of the app server -->
```

In this example, we use logic to branch off to the appropriate version of a target. This feels natural but is hard to express so clearly in an XML-based language. XML was intended to be used to represent data in the first place. Logic doesn't work so well. Besides that, Ant has a declarative language. You need to relinquish some control over the file and let Ant execute tasks in the right order—with a little guidance. Each target in the Ant file declares its dependencies using the depends attribute in the target declaration. If you feel the need to do any kind of branching in your build file, this indicates you may want to rearrange your build file.

This technique is especially powerful if you have many if-else elements in your build; you can take half a dozen branching constructs and distill them all down to a very cleanly delineated pair of files. Developers who work with object-oriented code may recognize this as an example of polymorphism, in which the Ant build can have targets of the same name but different behavior depending on the context.

Ant has possessed an import task since version 1.6, and you can use this feature with properties to import the file that contains the behavior you need.

> ### ant-contrib
>
> The if element comes from the ant-contrib project, which adds some scripting capabilities to Ant. Both the original creator and maintainers of Ant believe that Ant shouldn't be a complete scripting language. Use ant-contrib with care!

Replace Call with Dependency

Summary: Let Ant manage the dependencies instead of explicitly invoking them.

`refactoring_before.xml`

```
<target name="imperative_build">
    <antcall target="compile"/>
    <antcall target="test"/>
</target>
```

⬇

`refactoring_after.xml`

```
<target name="declarative_build" depends="test, publish "/>
<target name="test" depends="compile"/>
```

The entire point of dependency-based build tools such as Ant is to prevent targets from being run more than once. antcall subverts the subtle declarative nature of Ant by executing tasks imperatively. It is often used to try to reuse a task by passing different parameters upon invocation. It's easy to run targets twice or more when you use antcall, especially if you mix depends and antcall inside the same build.

The correct thing to do is declare that the deploy target depends on compile and test. The test target has its own dependency on compilation. Ant is designed to resolve the tree of dependencies and execute them in the correct order. It will also attempt to execute in the order that you declared them, but don't count on this because it will adjust that order to satisfy dependencies.

Replace Literal with Property

Summary: Use a property to replace repeating literal values in your build file; use built-in Java and Ant properties for external values.

Environment Variable

One common smell is the use of imported environment variables to find out what the username is or what the running OS is. Although this works, it's another external dependency on the build system, and this can make systems fragile. Java's system properties are included by default in an Ant build's namespace. So instead of importing the environment and then trying to derive things from entries that you find, use the built-in properties where you can: user.name, os.name, and so on.

`refactoring_before.xml`

```xml
<target name="deploy_to_tomcat">
    <copy file="dist.dir/webapp.war" todir="tomcat.webapps.dir"/>
</target>
```

⬇

`refactoring_after.xml`

```xml
<property name="dist.dir" location="${build.dir}/dist"/>
<property name="tomcat.webapps.dir" location="/opt/tomcat5/webapps"/>
<target name="deploy_to_tomcat">
    <copy file="${dist.dir}/webapp.war" todir="${tomcat.webapps.dir}"/>
</target>
```

It's necessary to use properties to represent static and dynamic strings in your build. The directory that you compile classes to may not change often, but when it does, you want to make one change, rather than five. As a rule of thumb, if you find yourself typing the same string three times, you should make a property. See "Replace Value Attribute with Location" for more about how to represent filesystem paths in properties. It's always worth remembering that properties are immutable in Ant. So, the first value to be assigned to the property sticks to the property. This means you can override the property outside the build if you want or introduce default values in a property file in a file that is evaluated last.

Introduce filtersfile

Summary: Use a property file to map elements to values, and refer to the properties directly in your template rather than via a set of elements.

refactoring_before.xml

```
<target name="filter">
        <copy todir="${build}" file="${src}/config/config.xml">
            <filterset>
                <filter token="APP_SERVER_PORT" value="${appserver.port}"/>
                <filter token="APP_SERVER_HOST" value="${appserver.host}"/>
                <filter token="APP_SERVER_USERID" value="${appserver.userid}"/>
                </filterset>
        </copy>
</target>
```

⬇

refactoring_after.xml

```
<target name="filtersfile">
    <copy todir="${build}" file="${src}/config/config.xml">
        <filterset filtersfile="appserver.properties"/>
      </copy>
</target>
```

appserver.properties

```
appserver.port=8080
appserver.host=oberon
appserver.userid=beamish
# END filtersfile
```

Build files can quickly become difficult to read. Properties are sometimes best kept in a plain-text file where any member of the project team
can see and understand them. This example demonstrates this technique in the context of filtersets. Many build systems replace tokens in
templates with values, especially when you need to maintain files for
different environments. If you don't already reuse filterset elements by
ID, you'll find that they can dominate the build file with large blocks
of tokens. This approach has two benefits; you don't need to introduce
a token for a value (you can directly use the property name), and you
get to expose a property file that anyone can edit without making your
XML invalid. You can use more than one filtersfile value as a child of
the copy element as well. They are evaluated on a first-come first-served
basis, so values can have defaults. The filters file is a plain properties
file, which can be used elsewhere in your build.

Introduce Property File

Summary: Move infrequently changing properties out of the main build
and into a file.

> ### How Many Properties Should You Have Anyway?
>
> Too few, and you end you end up with unattractive concatenations of properties, a violation of the Don't Repeat Yourself (DRY) rule; too many, and you end up having duplicate properties or too many to keep in mind. If you can divide your build into different files, you can try to scope properties by file.

`refactoring_before.xml`

```
<property name="appserver.port" value="8080" />
<property name="appserver.host" value="oberon" />
<property name="appserver.userid" value="beamish" />
```

⬇

`refactoring_after.xml`

```
<property file="appserver.properties" />
```

`appserver.properties`

```
appserver.port=8080
appserver.host=oberon
appserver.userid=beamish
# END filtersfile
```

Ant doesn't recognize entities like constants in a build file; there's no point because all properties are immutable in any case. The main difference that you may encounter is that some properties are fixed; in addition, some are dynamically created perhaps on invocation in Ant or as an output of a task. Those static properties are the closest thing we have to constants, and it is those that you can remove from your Ant file and evaluate via a properties file. This does make your build.xml more legible, although you may trade some of the visibility of the properties as you push them down into a file.

Move Target to Wrapper Build File

Summary: Pull CI targets out of the developer build file; provide some indirection.

refactoring_before.xml

```
<target name="build">
        <!-- developer build-->
    </target>
 <target name="functest">
        <!-- functional tests-->
 </target>


<target name="cruise" depends="update,build,tag"/>
<target name="functional_cruise" depends="update,build,functest,tag"/>
```

⬇

refactoring_after.xml

```
<target name="build">
    <!-- developer build-->
</target>
<target name="functest">
    <!-- functional tests-->
</target>
```

ccbuild.xml

```
<project name="cruise" default="tag">

    <target name="tag" depends="build">
        <!-- code to tag the files you have checked out -->
    </target>

    <target name="build" depends="update">
        <ant buildfile="build.xml"/>
    </target>

    <target name="update" >
        <!-- code to update from your scm system-->
    </target>

</project>
<!-- END ccbuild  -->


<project  default="update" basedir=".."
        xmlns:my="antlib:com.thoughtworks.monkeybook">
    <target name="update" depends="build">
        <my:svn_up/>
    </target>
</project>
<!-- END antlibccbuild  -->
```

Continuous integration is a technique for reducing integration pain on software projects. Every time a developer commits source code changes to the source control repository, the CI server will check out the newest version of the code, compile it, and run tests. There are many ways to notify the team of changes in status (audible warnings are great for a colocated team), and there should be a strong cultural bias to keeping the build in a green or passing state. If two developers work on code that doesn't integrate, the team will know quickly.

CI operations (for example, SCM tagging, updates, and so on) can sometimes become very tightly coupled to your build. Ideally, the CI system should run the identical build to the developer, with any extra targets being in a wrapper Ant file that calls down to the developer build, using the ant task. If you run several CI builds on the same codebase, you can maintain several ccbuilds and keep all the mechanics of CI out of harm's way in these files.

Replace Comment with Description

Summary: Apply descriptions to tags rather than inline comments.

`refactoring_before.xml`

```
<target name="distribute">
        <!-- copy the compiled classes -->
    <copy todir="${dist}">
        <fileset dir="${classes.dir}"/>
    </copy>
</target>
```

⬇

`refactoring_after.xml`

```
<target name="dist">
        <copy todir="${dist}" description="copy compiled classes">
        <fileset dir="${classes.dir}"/>
    </copy>
</target>
```

Many Ant build files are peppered with comments. Comments can be a good thing, but they can also obscure the mechanics of the build. Almost all tasks accept a description attribute; so, you can directly annotate a task rather than introduce a comment near it. You could also use the taskname attribute to tell the user what is happening at runtime. I like to keep the task names short, so keep the long explanations to the descriptions.

Push Deployment Code into Import

Summary: The targets that deploy your code should be in a separate file from the targets your developers use.

A Good Likeness

Having said all that, try to deploy to as lifelike a stack as you can. Choose your lightweight container wisely.

`refactoring_before.xml`
```
<target name="deploy_to_weblogic" >
    <!-- insert WL task or similar -->
    <sshexec host="${deploy.host}" username="dev" command="restart_container"/>
</target>
```

⬇

`refactoring_after.xml`
```
<import file="deploy.xml" />
<target name="test_in_container" depends="deploy_to_weblogic"/>
```

If all projects used a single application server on a single host, it would be simple to have one build file. But it's common to use more than one application server on a project, such as a lightweight server on the developer's desktop and an enterprise one in the data center.

If you extract the relevant code for each to a separate file, you get a nice separation of concerns. You can import whatever file you need, and all the details of deploying to everything else are hidden. Also, you can significantly simplify your final project object that Ant builds when it parses the build files, so the fact that you are missing some of the dependencies for a local build isn't a problem when you want to deploy to an enterprise server.

Move Element to antlib

Summary: Take Ant build elements that are repeated across many projects and distribute via an antlib.

`ccbuild.xml`
```
<project name="cruise" default="tag">

    <target name="tag" depends="build">
        <!-- code to tag the files you have checked out -->
    </target>
```

```
<target name="build" depends="update">
    <ant buildfile="build.xml"/>
</target>

<target name="update" >
    <!-- code to update from your scm system-->
</target>

</project>
<!-- END ccbuild  -->

<project  default="update" basedir="."
        xmlns:my="antlib:com.thoughtworks.monkeybook">
    <target name="update" depends="build">
        <my:svn_up/>
    </target>
</project>
<!-- END antlibccbuild  -->
```

⬇

`ccbuild.xml`

```
<project  default="update" basedir="."
        xmlns:my="antlib:com.thoughtworks.monkeybook">
    <target name="update" depends="build">
        <my:svn_up/>
    </target>
</project>
<!-- END antlibccbuild  -->
```

`antlib.xml`

```
<antlib>
    <macrodef name="svn_up">
        <attribute name="svn.exe" default="/usr/bin/svn" />
        <sequential>
            <echo message="${basedir}" />
            <exec failonerror="true" executable="@{svn.exe}">
                <arg value="update" />
            </exec>
        </sequential>
    </macrodef>
</antlib>
<!-- END antlib-->
```

Ant-based projects often repeat the same literal blocks of Ant XML code again and again. This is one of the factors that led to the creation of the Maven project: "While there were some common themes across the separate builds, each community was creating its own build systems

> ### Where Is Each Library Used?
> If you make subdirectories for runtime and build-time libraries, it's a good start. Knowing whether something is required for build or deploy is very useful.

and there was no reuse of build logic across projects" [Casey]. antlib is an XML file with a root element of antlib. When this file is in your classpath (perhaps bundled as a JAR file in your $ANT_HOME/lib directory) and you specify an XML namespace for your build file, you can directly access the elements defined. Here's a real-world example:

For example, on large projects you may end up with dozens of smaller projects being built by CruiseControl. Each one of these projects needs to do the following:

- Update the checkout from source control.

- Invoke the developer build.

- Tag the codebase if the build passes.

Each build will have a short build file (possibly called cc-build.xml or similar) that does these operations before calling down to the developer build. antlib allows you to expose types, tasks, and macrodefs via the default classpath. So, for the example project, you can declare an SVN task or macrodef and put it in the $ANT_HOME/lib directory, so everybody or everything using your default Ant distribution can use common types. You'll need to do some work to package it for use by the rest of the team.

```
mkdir -p com/thoughtworks/monkeybook/
cp ~/workspace/monkeybook/content/antlib.xml com/thoughtworks/monkeybook/.
jar cvf antlib.jar com
cp /tmp/antlib.jar apache-ant-1.6.5/lib/.
```

Once the JAR file is in the project's classpath, you can use the macrodef as in the earlier example.

Replace Large Library Definitions with a Fileset

Summary: Use a nested fileset inside your path definition rather than painstakingly specifying your path elements by hand.

`refactoring_before.xml`

```
<path id="build.path">
    <pathelement location="${lib}/build/junit.jar"/>
    <pathelement location="${lib}/build/crimson.jar"/>
    <pathelement location="${lib}/build/emma.jar"/>
</path>
```

⬇

`refactoring_after.xml`

```
<path id="build.path">
 <fileset dir="${lib}/build" />
</path>
```

In most projects, libraries get checked into source control. It can be tedious to update references to libraries as they change. This example doesn't have version numbers in the path, but if you want to upgrade a library one point release, you have to change your build. Letting Ant discover your libraries does a lot of the work for you, but beware: you still need to understand what libraries your code uses and organize them in the right way.

Move Runtime Properties

Summary: Keep runtime properties distinct from your build properties so that you can reconfigure your application easily.

`refactoring_before.xml`

```
<target name="war">
    <copy file="${src}/runtime.properties"
        tofile="${build}/war/lib/myapp.properties"/>
    <war destfile="${dist}/myapp.war" basedir="${build}/war"/>
</target>
```

⬇

`refactoring_after.xml`

```
<property name="runtime.smtp.server" value="foo.thoughtworks.com"/>
<property name="web.service.endpoint" value="bar.thoughtworks.com/axis"/>
<target name="war">
    <echoproperties destfile="${build}/war/lib/myapp.properties"/>
    <war destfile="${dist}/myapp.war" basedir="${build}/war"/>
</target>
```

Do you need to repackage or even recompile your application to deploy to a different environment? You should be able to compile your release candidates and park them in a repository to be deployed at some later

---

Free the Configuration

Once your build starts to get slow and/or you get closer to release, consider unbundling the configuration from the code. There will come a time where you want to change a configuration property without redeploying. You can deploy runtime property files to the filesystem, for example. This works well because you can edit them when you need to, although in a production environment you'll need to make sure they are secured. LDAP is another possibility (although more work), and you may introduce another service that your application depends on.

---

stage; that ensures you are always deploying the same code that you tested earlier. Another problem we have seen is the need to rebuild applications in order to change trivial properties that the application uses at runtime ("Web services endpoint URL changed? You need to rebuild.").

There are two very different sets of properties in your build: build time (where to compile to and what repository to publish to) and runtime (what database credentials to use and external service information). It's easy to get these runtime and buildtime properties mixed up, with much hilarity. This doesn't often cause issues until you start to merge properties back and forth between code branches as environments change or until you need to wait for twenty minutes of automated functional tests to pass so you can get a release candidate with your single property change in it.

Properties can get out of control if you don't manage them throughout the life cycle of a software project; do yourself a favor, and separate them into different buckets—those properties needed to create the artifact of a deployable application and the configuration properties needed to run that application. Consider moving the runtime properties to their own repository so they are independent of a particular build of code, project, or team.

Reuse Elements by ID

Summary: Replace duplicated elements such as paths and sets with a reference to a single instance of that element.

`refactoring_before.xml`

```xml
<target name="copy_and_filter">
   <copy todir="${build}/content">
      <fileset dir="${html}" />
      <filterset>
         <filter token="AUTHOR" value="${author.name}" />
         <filter token="DATE" value="${timestamp}" />
         <filter token="COPYRIGHT" value="${copyright.txt}" />
      </filterset>
   </copy>
   <copy todir="${build}/abstracts">
      <fileset dir="${abstracts}" />
      <filterset>
         <filter token="AUTHOR" value="${author.name}" />
         <filter token="DATE" value="${timestamp}" />
         <filter token="COPYRIGHT" value="${copyright.txt}" />
      </filterset>
   </copy>
</target>
```

⬇

`refactoring_after.xml`

```xml
<filterset id="publishing_filters">
   <filter token="AUTHOR" value="${author.name}" />
   <filter token="DATE" value="${timestamp}" />
   <filter token="COPYRIGHT" value="${copyright.txt}" />
</filterset>

<target name="copy_and_filter">
   <copy todir="${build}/content">
      <fileset dir="${html.content}" />
      <filterset refid="publishing_filters"/>
   </copy>
   <copy todir="${build}/abstracts">
      <fileset dir="${abstracts}" />
      <filterset refid="publishing_filters"/>
   </copy>
</target>
```

Many top-level elements such as path, filterset, and fileset allow the author to call them by reference. Instead of duplicating a path, you can declare it once, assign an ID to it, and then refer to that element throughout the rest of the build.xml file. This is particularly useful when confronted with a large build.xml file from a busy project; the sheer number of lines in the file can make it hard to understand the intent behind it, and collapsing many path or filterset declarations into a single line is a nice gumption-boosting activity that allows you to get traction.

You may also find a bug, such as if somebody forgot to update all the instances of a filterset in a big build.xml file.

Move Property Outside Target

Summary: Move properties that are declared in a target to the body of the build file.

`refactoring_before.xml`

```xml
<target name="distribute">
    <property name="dist_file" value="widget-1.0.tar"/>
    <tar destfile="${dist_file}">
            <tarfileset dir="${build}/dist"/>
    </tar>
    <gzip src="${dist_file}"/>
    <scp file="${dist_file}.gz"
        todir="${appserver.userid}@${appserver.host}:/tmp"/>
 </target>
```

⬇

`refactoring_after.xml`

```xml
<property name="dist_file" value="widget-1.0.tar"/>
 <target name="distribute">
    <tar destfile="${dist_file}">
            <tarfileset dir="${build}/dist"/>
    </tar>
    <gzip src="${dist_file}"/>
    <scp file="${dist_file}.gz"
        todir="${appserver.userid}@${appserver.host}:/tmp"/>
   </target>
```

Many of us know how to make a variable local to a block of code. It's lexical scoping, and it doesn't exist in Ant. If you declare a property, it is immediately available to any task or target in your project namespace. It's a tempting idea to declare properties where they are used, but don't think you have scoped the property to the target.

What can really start to confuse your colleagues is if they use the same property names; the value of a property may then change depending on the execution order of the targets. It is possible, using the ant-contrib library, to break the fundamentally immutable nature of a property. This can lead to your project using Ant as a scripting language rather than a build tool.

Replace Value Element with Location

`refactoring_before.xml`

```
<property name="libdir" value="lib" />
<property name="libdir.runtime" value="${libdir}/runtime" />
```

⬇

`refactoring_after.xml`

```
<property name="libdir" location="lib" />
<property name="libdir.runtime" location="${libdir}/runtime" />
```

Your Ant build may work if you run it from a certain directory or with a certain environment variable set. You may even have a wiki page that tells a new developer how to get set up and how to build their environment.

Ideally, however, your build.xml file should tell the user what it needs, if it can't find out for itself. Using the location attribute on a property element is the first step toward achieving this goal of a robust build. People will misuse your scripts and tools; try to accommodate the common misuse cases so that running something as the wrong user will immediately cause the program to exit with a nice error message. Ant generally does the right thing when you invoke it from the wrong directory; by default, it sets a ${basedir} property to be the directory where the build.xml file is installed. Ant constructs properties set with a location attribute to be relative to the ${basedir} directory and will do the right thing by setting the path to be fully qualified to the directory your build.xml file is residing in, rather than a relative path. A lot of builds use the value attribute in properties, which can lead to brittle builds.

You can use the location attribute in other kinds of elements as well, most notably the arg element passed to tasks such as execute. These work in the same way, providing an accurate path to the task.

Push Wrapper Script into build.xml File

Summary: Move path and option scripts back down into the build file.

`go.bat`

```
@echo off

set CLASSPATH=%CLASSPATH%;lib\crimson.jar
set CLASSPATH=%CLASSPATH%;lib\jaxp.jar
set CLASSPATH=%CLASSPATH%;lib\ojdbc14.jar
```

```
cd build
ant -f build.xml
rem END push_down_wrappers
```

```
refactoring_after.xml
<classpath id="classpath" description="The default classpath.">
  <pathelement path="${classpath}"/>
  <fileset dir="lib">
    <include name="jaxp.jar"/>
    <include name="crimson.jar"/>
    <include name="ojdbc14.jar"/>
  </fileset>
</classpath>
```

Many projects end up generating DOS batch, Unix shell, or Perl wrappers to the Ant build. These usually contain project-specific information and perhaps some options; they are sometimes used to provide a friendly front end to complicated project builds so that anybody can build the code. They also tend to get wrapped in other scripts. It can be frustrating trying to debug these, so try to avoid using them where possible, or just use a one-line script if necessary. They can also have the unintended consequence of never passing return codes up to the calling process. This can mask problems if your automated deployment process calls an Ant script and then does something else.

To make your build more robust, you can use the fail element to do a preflight check and make sure that all your properties are set correctly. In conjunction with fail, you can use the available task to signal via a property that files, classpath entries, or JVM resources are obtainable by your Ant process. You can also use -D options on the command line to create properties that you might need.

If you're getting fed up with typing in the command line or you get complaints from the rest of the team, then by all means do create a wrapper script like go.bat, but keep it to one or two lines—just enough to get you from your operating system's shell into Ant. For extra credit on Windows systems, you might unset the CLASSPATH environment variable so it doesn't pollute the build's classpath. Many Windows installer packages will append or prepend entries to the CLASSPATH environment variable, giving unpredictable results on some workstations.

Sometimes, however, you'll need to make some libraries available to Ant for it to execute some tasks. The Ant manual lists those tasks that have external library dependencies.

> ### Calling Ant
>
> Ant's invocation script will reliably give a nonzero exit code on Unix systems if the build fails. Don't assume that you'll get the same thing on Windows systems, because the ant.bat file notably doesn't return a Windows error-level value on some versions of Ant. There are also some dynamic language wrappers to Ant; you're best to test these also to make sure that a failed build will stop your deploy script from keeping on trucking.

To satisfy those dependencies, you *could* use a wrapper script with a list of libraries to add to the classpath, or you could put the libraries in Ant's lib directory. When Ant is invoked, it calls a launcher class to generate a classpath from the libraries it finds. This is a convenient way to satisfy library dependencies. It's also a good idea to check this copy of Ant into source control so everybody can check it out and run the build, without setting up their computers for the project.

Add taskname Attribute

Summary: Make Ant display meaningful output for the task so you can understand the intent of the code.

`refactoring_before.xml`

```xml
<target name="copy_config">
    <copy tofile="${output}/style.xsl" file="${src}/xsl/style.xsl" />
    <copy todir="${output}">
            <fileset dir="${xml.docs}"/>
    </copy>
    <copy todir="${output}/images">
        <fileset dir="${common}/images"/>
    </copy>
</target>
```

⬇

`refactoring_after.xml`

```xml
<target name="copy_config">
    <copy tofile="${output}/style.xsl"
        file="${src}/xsl/style.xsl" taskname="copy xsl stylesheet"/>
    <copy todir="${output}" taskname="copy xml docs to output">
        <fileset dir="${xml.docs}"/>
        </copy>
        <copy todir="${output}/images" taskname="copy images to output">
        <fileset dir="${common}/images"/>
        </copy>
</target>
```

Sometimes you end up writing a build that executes the same task several times in a row; copy is a good example of this. It can be hard for the users of your build file to see what the build is doing in this situation. It helps greatly if you add a task name to the task so that it's clear what you are trying to achieve.

Enforce Internal Target

Summary: Make the first character of internal target names a hyphen so they cannot be called from the command line.

`refactoring_before.xml`

```
<target name="init">
    <mkdir dir="build"/>
</target>
```

⬇

`refactoring_after.xml`

```
<target name="-init">
    <mkdir dir="build"/>
</target>
```

Calling the wrong target may have unintended consequences for your build, especially if you never intended the target to be run from the command line. Because there is no way to declare a task private like you might create a private method in Java code, someone thought up this simple but clever idea: fool Ant into treating the target like a command-line option. The shell passes it to the Ant wrapper script as a positional parameter, and Ant itself parses arguments with a leading hyphen as an option. So, it has no choice but to try to evaluate a task like -create_database as an option, which doesn't exist. You may confuse matters if you have an internal target called -propertyfile or -logger, however.

Move Outputs Directory to Parent

Summary: Take components that are built from many places and centralize them under one directory.

```
project/
|-- build
|-- dist
|-- docs
|-- src
`-- testresults
```

```
project/
|-- build
|    |-- dist
|    |-- docs
|    `-- testresults
`-- src
```

If you have many directories that could be dynamically updated by your code, things get confusing. You have to clean several directories to start from scratch, you cherry-pick pieces from one directory to drop to another, and your life is more complicated. Pick one directory as the place where things are generated, make sure that your source control system will ignore generated files, and start migrating all built artifacts there. If your properties refer to a canonical location, moving the directory becomes a one-line change.

Replace Exec with Apply

`refactoring_before.xml`

```xml
<exec executable="md5sum" output="md5sums.txt">
        <arg value="${dist.dir}/foo.dll"/>
        <arg value="${dist.dir}/bar.dll"/>
</exec>
```

`refactoring_after.xml`

```xml
<apply executable="md5sum" output="md5sums.txt">
        <fileset dir="${dist.dir}" includes="*.dll"/>
</apply>
```

Exec has a limited set of arguments that you can apply and is really meant for simple commands. Apply allows you to exec something on an Ant type, which means you can pass filesets, with refids, and so on. Much cleaner.

Use CI Publishers

Summary: Don't let a failed tag break the build; it impedes the developer feedback cycle.

`refactoring_before.xml`

```xml
<target name="cruisecontrol" depends="developer_build, functional_tests, tag">
```

```
refactoring_after.xml
```

```xml
<target name="cruisecontrol" depends="developer_build, functional_tests">

<target name="tag"
    description="this will fail unless run from a cruise publisher">
    <fail unless="logdir"
        message="${logdir} property missing -
        are you running this from a cruisecontrol publisher"/>
</target>
```

Introduce Distinct Target Naming

Summary: Use a style so that targets and properties don't have the same naming conventions.

```
refactoring_before.xml
```

```xml
<property name="build.dir" location="${basedir}/build"/>
<property name="lib.dir" location="${basedir}/build"/>
<target name="test.unit" >
    <junit haltonerror="false" haltonfailure="false">
        <!-- details excluded -->
    </junit>
</target>
```

⬇

```
refactoring_after.xml
```

```xml
<property name="build.dir" location="${basedir}/build"/>
<property name="lib.dir" location="${basedir}/build"/>
    <target name="unit-test" >
            <junit haltonerror="false" haltonfailure="false">
                <!-- details excluded -->
            </junit>
    </target>
```

"... Something about the nature of Ant itself makes people treat it very differently from the code it's building. Rules concerning consistency, testing, maintainability and even common sense seem to go out the window" [Newman]. XML isn't necessarily easy to read. build.xml files need as much help as they can get to stay legible. In practice, this means sticking to a style for build.xml files. What quickly bugs the reader is using the same style of separating words with dots for targets and properties. It's not always clear when an attribute might refer to a property and when it may refer to a value. Consider using dots to separate words in properties, because Java properties use dots, and the namespace of Java system properties is included in your Ant project's. Underscores or dashes work nicely for target names. See "The Elements of Ant Style"[1] for more. Some of the advice isn't required anymore; for example, modern IDEs help you navigate through Ant files instead of needing to add blocks of comments to identify targets. Also, tools such as Grand (see the "Resources" section for more information) will help you visualize your build dependency tree.

Rename Target with Noun

Summary: Name your targets with the article that they produce instead of the process of producing them.

refactoring_before.xml

```
<target name="foo-build-webapp">
    <war destfile="foo.war">
      <fileset dir="${build.dir}/frontend/dist"/>
    </war>
</target>
```

⬇

refactoring_after.xml

```
<target name="foo.war">
    <war destfile="foo.war">
      <fileset dir="${build.dir}/frontend/dist"/>
    </war>
</target>
```

"I recommend choosing names describing what they produce, e.g., classes, test/report." [Williams]

There is a an idiom in Ant build.xml files that you should have a "compile" target, a "test" target, and so on. There's a certain logic in this. Sometimes you want just to run a target that represents a state. This could be ready to deploy, ready to publish, or something similar. Where your build produces artifacts, you can focus on that artifact. There's also the possibility of using the uptodate task to skip running targets that don't need to be run, saving everyone time. This also greatly enhances the clarity of the build.

You might have seen this before if you used any of the make family. The generally accepted make style is to name targets after the artifact they produce. What you gain in ease of use, you lose in platform independence unfortunately.

---

1. http://wiki.apache.org/ant/TheElementsOfAntStyle

11.3 Summary

This essay introduced refactoring to Ant build files. Some of the refactorings are directly translated from the original Refactoring book [FBB⁺99]; others are gathered from the field. It can be hard to get started when confronted with an existing build that you want to change, but your effort will pay off. Don't lose sight of the fact that you build software to deploy to production. If you're constantly evaluating your build in that context, you might just have a good go-live weekend.

11.4 References

[Hunt, Thomas]	*The Pragmatic Programmer*
[Newman]	http://www.magpiebrain.com/blog/2004/12/15/ant-and-the-use-of-the-full-stop/
[Casey]	*Better Builds with Maven*
[Fowler, Foemmel]	http://martinfowler.com/articles/continuousIntegration.html
[Loughran, Hatcher]	*Java Development with Ant*

11.5 Resources

Grand: www.ggtools.net/grand

The Elements of Ant Style: wiki.apache.org/ant/TheElementsOfAntStyle

Chapter 12

Single-Click Software Release

by Dave Farley, Technology Principal

12.1 Continuous Build

A core practice in agile development projects is the use of continuous integration (CI). CI is a process by which builds and extensive suites of automated test cases are run at the point that software is committed to the version control system.

This practice has been in use on projects for many years and provides a high degree of security that at any given point the software under development will successfully build and pass its unit-test suite. This significantly increases confidence that the software serves its purpose. For many, and some would say most, projects, this is a huge step forward in the quality and reliability of the software ultimately delivered.

In complex projects, though, the potential for problems doesn't stop at the point at which the code will compile and pass unit tests.

However good the unit test coverage, it is, by its nature, closer to the solution of the problem than the requirements. In some circumstances, unit tests can get into a state where they prove only that the solution is the same solution that the development team envisaged, rather than that it is one that fulfills the requirements.

Once the code is built, it must be deployed, and for most modern software built by teams of developers, this is not a simple case of copying a single binary to the file system. Instead, it often involves deploying and configuring a collection of technical pieces, web servers, databases, application servers, queues, and others in addition to the software itself.

Such software usually has to go through a reasonably complex release process, visiting a variety of deployed environments on its progress toward production. It will be deployed to development machines, QA environments, performance test environments, and production staging environments before finally making it into production.

In most projects, most, if not all, of these steps will include a significant degree of manual intervention. People will manually manage configuration files, and they will manually tailor the deployment to suit the environment to which it is being deployed. There is always something to forget. "It took me two hours to find that the development environment stores its template files in a different location than production."

Continuous integration helps, but in its most common incarnation it is misnamed; it should be called "continuous build." What if it really did apply to the whole release process? What if it really was a continuous integration of the entire system?

12.2 Beyond Continuous Build

The teams I have been working on have been taking this to heart for the past couple of years and have been building end-to-end continuous integration release systems that will deploy large, complex applications to whichever environment we choose at the click of a button. This approach has resulted in a dramatic reduction in stress at the point of release and a significant reduction in problems encountered. During the process of establishing these end-to-end CI environments, we have discovered a fairly general abstraction of the build process that helps us hit the ground running and allows us to build fairly sophisticated build systems rapidly at the start of our projects.

The process is based on the idea of a release candidate progressing through a series of gates. At each stage the confidence in the release candidate is enhanced. The objective of this approach is to develop this level of confidence in a release candidate to a point at which the system is proven ready for release into production. True to agile development principles, this process is started with every check-in, with every check-in, in effect, being a viable release candidate in its own right.

As the release candidate proceeds through the process, some of the gates through which the release candidate may pass are essential to most projects, and some are more tailored to meet the needs of a specific project.

We commonly refer to this process, this sequence of gates, as a *build pipeline*, *pipelined build*, or *continuous integration pipeline*. It has also been referred to as a *staged build*.

12.3 Full Lifecycle Continuous Integration

You can see a typical full lifecycle in Figure 12.1, on page 171. This is a continuous integration pipeline that captures the essence of the approach. This process has proven, through experience on a number of different projects, to be fairly generic, although it is, as with all agile practices, normally tailored and tuned to meet specific project needs.

The process starts with the developers committing changes into a source code repository. The CI system, typically CruiseControl on our projects, responds to the commit by triggering the CI process. In this case, it compiles the code, runs commit tests, and, if they all pass, creates assemblies[1] of the compiled code and commits these assemblies to a managed area of storage.

Managing Binaries

A fundamental of this approach is that each step in the process should move the release candidate forward in its progress toward full release. One important reason for this is that we want to minimize the opportunities for errors to creep into the process.

For example, when we store source code only, we have to recompile that source code each time we want to deploy. If we are about to run a performance test and need to first recompile the source code, then we run the risk of something being different in the performance test environment; perhaps we inadvertently used a different version of the compiler or linked with a different version of a library. We want to eliminate, as far as we can, the possibility of inadvertently introducing errors that we should have found at the commit test or functional test stages of the build pipeline.

This philosophy of avoiding rework within the process has several side benefits. It tends to keep the scripts for each step in the process very

---

1. In this instance, assemblies are any grouping of compiled code; these will be .NET assemblies, Java JARs, WAR files, and EAR files. A key point is that these assemblies do not include configuration information. We want the same binary to be runnable in any environment.

simple, and it encourages a clean separation of environment-specific stuff and environment-neutral stuff.[2]

However, care needs to be taken when managing binaries in this manner. It is too easy to waste vast amounts of storage on binaries that are rarely if ever used. In most cases, we compromise. We avoid storing such binaries in version control systems, because the overhead is simply not worth the benefits. Instead, we have started using a dedicated area of a shared filesystem. We manage this as a rolling binary repository, archiving binaries into version-labeled, compressed images. So far we have written our own scripts for this stuff, not yet having found a suitable off-the-shelf alternative.

These binary images are tagged with the version information of the source code from which they were built. It is easiest to think of the build tag as a release candidate identifier; it is used to represent the association between all the source code, all the binaries, and all the configuration information, scripts, and anything else it takes to build and deploy the system.

This collection of "managed binaries" represents a cache of recent builds. Past a certain point we delete the old binaries. If we later decide that we need to step back to a version for which the binaries have been removed, we must rerun the whole pipelined build for that source tag, which remains safely in the version control system, but this is a very rare event.

12.4 The Check-in Gate

The automated build pipeline is initiated by creating a release candidate. This candidate is created implicitly when any developer commits any change to the version control system.

At this point, code will be compiled, and a series of commit tests will be run. This collection of commit tests will normally include all unit tests, plus a small selection of smoke tests, plus any other tests that prove that this check-in does indeed represent a viable release candidate, one that is worth the time to evaluate further.

2. The process implicitly discourages the compilation of binaries for specific deployment targets. Such deployment-target-specific binaries are the antithesis of flexible deployment yet are common in enterprise systems.

The objective of these commit tests is to fail fast. The check-in gate is interactive; the developers are waiting for a pass before proceeding to their next task. In view of this, speed is of the essence to maintain the efficiency of the development process.

However, failures later in the CI pipeline are more expensive to fix, so a judicious selection of additions to the commit test suite, beyond the essential unit tests, is often valuable in maintaining the efficiency of the team.

Once the commit tests have all passed, we consider that the check-in gate has been passed. Developers are now free to move on to other tasks, even though later stages in the build pipeline have yet to run, let alone pass.

This is more than anything else a process-level optimization. In an ideal world where all acceptance tests, performance tests, and integration tests will run in a matter of seconds, there is no advantage to pipelining the CI process. However, in the real world, these tests always take a long time to run, and it would be a massive blow to the productivity of a development team to have to wait until all had completed successfully before being able to continue.

Treating the commit test build as a check-in gate frees the team to move on with new tasks. However, the team is expected to closely monitor the outcome of the release candidate that results from their check-in through the rest of its life cycle. The objective is for the team to catch errors as soon as it can and fix them, while allowing them to get on with other work in parallel with lengthy test runs.

This approach is acceptable only when the commit test coverage is sufficiently good to catch most errors. If most errors are being caught at later stages in the pipeline, it is a good signal that it is time to beef up your commit tests!

As developers, we will always argue for the fastest commit cycle. In reality, this need must be balanced with the check-in gate's ability to identify the most common errors we are likely to introduce. This is an optimization process that can work only through trial and error.

Start the design of your commit test suite by running all unit tests, and later add specific tests to try to trap common failures that you see occurring in later stages of the pipeline.

12.5   The Acceptance Test Gate

Unit tests are an essential part of any agile development process, but they are rarely enough on their own. It is not uncommon to have an application where all unit tests pass but where the application doesn't meet the requirements of the business it was developed to serve.

In addition to unit tests, and the slightly broader category of commit tests, the teams I work with rely heavily on automated acceptance tests. These tests capture the acceptance criteria of the stories we develop and prove that the code meets those acceptance criteria.

These are functional tests; that is, they exercise the system end to end, though often with the exception of any interactions with external systems outside our control. In those cases, we generally stub such external connection points for the purposes of our acceptance test suite.

We like to bring the creation and maintenance of these acceptance tests into the heart of our development process, with no story deemed complete until its acceptance criteria are tested by an automated suite created by the developers and added to the acceptance test suite. We tend to expend some energy on ensuring such tests are very readable, even to nontechnical people, but that is perhaps less fundamental to our CI process and so is outside the scope of this essay.

Acceptance tests are run in a controlled environment dedicated to the task and are monitored by our CI management system (usually Cruise-Control).

The acceptance test gate is a second key point in the life cycle of a release candidate. Our automated deployment system will deploy only those release candidates that have passed all acceptance tests. This means that it is not possible to progress any release candidate beyond this stage into production unless all acceptance criteria are met.

12.6   Preparing to Deploy

In some circumstances, it may make sense to automate the deployment of everything associated with an application, but for large-scale enterprise applications this is rarely the case. However, if we could automate the management and configuration of the entire infrastructure, it would eliminate the cause of many errors, specifically the manual deployment and configuration process so common in enterprise-scale systems. This

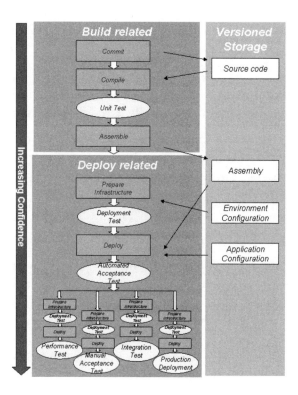

Figure 12.1: CONTINUOUS INTEGRATION PIPELINE

being the case, the attempt is worth some effort, and even if we partially succeed, we will usually eliminate many sources of common errors.

We have adopted a pragmatic approach to this problem, and we will often rely on a standard server image, application servers, message brokers, databases, and so on. These images will represent some form of "snapshot" of a deployed system installed and configured with a base-level configuration.

Such images can take many forms, whatever is needed or convenient for the project. Often we will have a database script that will establish a starting schema and a dump of data that will populate it. We may have standard OS installations or application-server configurations that can be deployed and established as part of the commissioning process for any server we decide to deploy to; it may even be as simple as a copy of a folder tree to a file system, so we always have the same structure in place.

Whatever the nature of the "image," the intent is to establish a common baseline configuration so that subsequent changes can be maintained as a collection of deltas from it.

Often we will maintain a collection of such images so that new environments can be set up quickly, leaving little room for human error.

This raw infrastructure is not deployed each time we deploy the software; in most cases, it is laid down at the point at which we commission some new environment and then rarely touched.

However, each time we deploy the application, we will reset the infrastructure to as close to this base state as is possible in order to establish a known-good starting point for the remainder of the deployment.

Once this baseline infrastructure is in place, it may prove helpful to run a suite of simple deployment tests. These tests are intended to confirm that the basic infrastructure is in place and ready to be configured to the specific needs of the application and specific environment. Typically these tests will be very simple and represent an assertion that the basic plumbing is in place, such as ensuring that the DBMS is present and the web server is responding to requests.

If these tests fail, we know that there is something wrong with our image or the hardware.

Once these tests pass, we know we are ready to deploy the application. The application-specific deployment scripts are run to copy our assemblies, which were built and tested during the commit stage of the process, from their area of managed storage to the correct locations.

In addition to simply copying binaries, our scripts will, where necessary, start and stop any application servers or web servers, populate databases with schemas or updates as appropriate, perhaps configure the message broker, and so on.

In essence, deployment is a five-stage process, with four stages for each individual deployment:

- A third-party infrastructure is installed, often from an image, where practicable. *This is done only at commissioning time for a new server environment.*

- The infrastructure is cleaned to a known-good start state.

- Deployment tests confirm the infrastructure is ready for the software.

- Application assemblies are deployed.

- The infrastructure is configured appropriately to the needs of the application.

We divide our build/deploy scripts into small pieces to keep them simple, as with any other well-factored software. Each is focused on a specific task and relies as much as possible on clearly defined inputs.

12.7 Subsequent Test Stages

As stated earlier, the acceptance test gate is a key milestone in the project life cycle. Once passed, the release candidate is available for deployment to any of a variety of systems. If the candidate fails this gate, it is effectively undeployable without significant manual effort; this is a good thing, because it maintains the discipline of releasing only that code that has been thoroughly tested and, as far as our automated test suite is able to, proven to work.

Progress through the continuous integration pipeline to this point has been wholly automated. If the release candidate has passed the previous stage of the process, it is promoted to the next stage, and that stage is run.

In most projects, that approach doesn't make sense for the remaining stages in the process, so instead we make the following stages optional, allowing any release candidate that has passed acceptance testing to be selected for deployment to either manual user acceptance testing, performance testing, or, indeed, deployment into production.

For each of these deployments, the steps described in the "Preparing to Deploy" section are performed, helping to ensure a clean deployment. By the time a release reaches production, it will have been successfully deployed using the same techniques several times, so there is little concern that anything will go wrong.

In my last project, each server that could host our application had a simple web page that provided a list of available release candidates and the ability to optionally rerun the functional test suite and/or the performance test suite in that environment. This provided a high degree of flexibility in our ability to deploy our system anytime we wanted to wherever we wanted with little fear of inadvertently introducing errors in the process.

The degree of automation involved, or not, in promoting release candidates through these subsequent stages is perhaps the most variable part of this otherwise fairly generic process. On some projects, it makes sense to always include a performance test run, and on others it may not. The details of the relationships between the different post-acceptance test stages and whether they are selected manually or run automatically is not really a problem, provided that the scripts managing the CI process are well factored.

12.8 Automating the Process

You'll see a simple map of the scripts used for the automation of a CI pipeline in Figure 12.2, on the facing page. Each box represents a process stage, and each line within a box represents an individual script, or build script target, that fulfills that function.

In most projects, using this approach, the first two process gates, check-in and acceptance, are initiated by a continuous integration management application such as CruiseControl.

One of the important benefits of this approach to organizing the build scripts is that each script, or script element, is focused on doing one, relatively straightforward thing well rather than trying to manage the entire build process in one complex step. This is a very important gain in ensuring that the build process is manageable and amenable to change as the project evolves and matures.

The details of these scripts are not within the scope of this essay and are, in reality, too project-dependant to be of much interest; however, we have found in a number of different projects that when we apply this kind of high-level structure to our build processes, we get reliable, repeatable, and trustworthy deployment, allowing us to deploy in seconds or minutes what previously took days—and often fraught weekend days at that!

12.9 Conclusion

If your organization is not yet using a CI approach to your build, start tomorrow. It is the most effective means of improving the reliability of your systems that we have found.

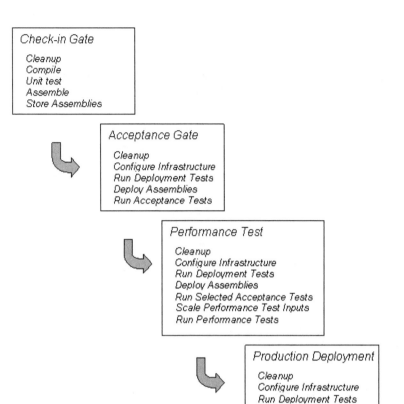

Figure 12.2: EXAMPLE PROCESS STEPS

Extending the range of CI to effectively eliminate as many sources of human error as possible has enormous benefits, not just in productivity but also in the quality of the deliverable and in lowering the stress of delivering into production.

Chapter 13

Agile vs. Waterfall Testing for Enterprise Web Apps

by Kristan Vingrys, QA Consultant

13.1 Introduction

How is the test strategy for an agile enterprise web application project different from the test strategy for one being developed using a waterfall process? Testing in either case focuses on informing business customers about what the application does. It also focuses on removing the risk of failure of the application once delivered into production. The main difference is not in the testing that is performed but in when the testing is performed and by whom. Test phases can start anytime the system is available and do not need to wait until a previous phase of testing has completed.

This essay is targeted at people either who have not been on an agile project before or who have just started an agile project and are looking for some guidance. The information isn't new, but it has been collected and presented to help you move in the direction of a more agile process.

The testing phases of an agile project are generally the same as a waterfall project. Exit criteria can still apply for each phase, but there is no longer a need to wait for the complete application to be finished before entering each testing phase. Instead, you wait only until enough of the application is completed to enter the next phase of testing. Because the testing is around functionality that is complete and not a release, testing phases are continually running in parallel. This results in a lot of regression testing, which means it is essential to automate the tests. Environment usage and resources are also a concern for a project that is agile because environments are needed earlier and more frequently.

"Fail fast" is a motto of agile projects, meaning try to determine that the application is not going to meet business requirements as soon as possible. To achieve this, you need to continually check and verify that the solution is satisfying the business need, and when it is not, you need to rectify the problem as soon as possible. An agile project team consists of developers, testers, architects, business analysts, and business representatives who are all concerned with delivering business value as early as possible. Therefore, testing is a concern of all team members and no longer just the responsibility of the tester.

13.2 Testing Life Cycle

The testing life cycle is where the biggest difference appears between waterfall and agile projects. Waterfall projects will have strict entry and exit criteria for each phase and move from one to the next only when the previous phase has finished. Agile projects will start a testing phase as soon as possible and allow them to overlap. There is still some structure to an agile project including exit criteria, but there is no strict entry criteria.

In Figure 13.1, on the next page, you can immediately see a difference between the testing life cycle for an agile project and that for a waterfall project. On an agile project, business analysts, test analysts, and business representatives discuss what the idea will do, how it fits into the bigger picture, and how to prove that it is doing what it should. This analysis forms the basis of the functional, user acceptance, and performance tests. It is after this analysis that the functionality is developed, which is when unit, integration, exploratory, and nonfunctional testing (and data validation if it is being performed) begins. Production verification occurs only once the system is about to go into production.

Not having strict entry criteria for a testing phase means it can begin at any time that is applicable. Because all test phases are important in ensuring the quality of an application, it is important to perform the analysis for each phase as soon as possible. Doing the test analysis early helps shape the design of the application and bring out issues, which can save significant time later in the project. Example exit criteria for an agile project are as follows.

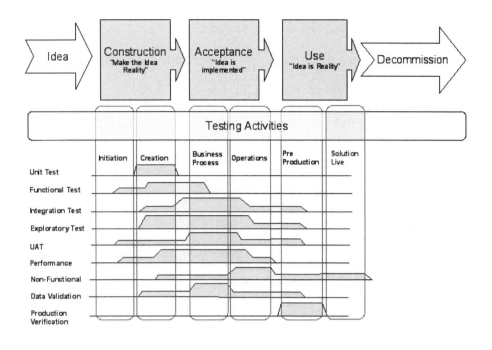

Figure 13.1: TESTING LIFE CYCLE FOR AN AGILE PROJECT AND WATERFALL PROJECT

Here are the criteria for unit testing:

- 100% automated
- 100% passing
- Greater than 90% code coverage
- Included in continuous build

Here are the criteria for integration testing:

- 100% automated
- 100% passing
- Included in continuous build

Here are the criteria for functional testing:

- Greater than 90% automated
- 100% passing
- All automated tests included in continuous build

Here is the criterion for exploratory testing:

- Confidence from test analysts that application is of good quality

Here are the criteria for user acceptance testing:

- Agreement from business representative that application satisfies need
- Agreement from users that application is usable

Here are the criteria for performance testing:

- 100% automated
- Agreement from business that application satisfies business performance requirements
- Performance tests are repeatable

Here are the criteria for nonfunctional testing:

- Agreement from business that nonfunctional requirements are met
- Agreement from operations that nonfunctional requirements are met

Here is the criterion for data validation testing:

- Confidence the data has been migrated correctly

Here is the criterion for production verification:

- Confidence the application has been installed correctly in the production environment

The testing life cycle of a waterfall project restricts the test phase that can be conducted until an earlier one has been completed. In theory, this makes sense because later test phases will rely on an earlier one passing (don't bother testing the performance of some functionality if it is not functionally correct). However, there is no reason to wait for all functionality to be correct before starting performance testing. An agile project will begin each test phase when it is appropriate, which results in issues being found early, giving the team more time to rectify the problems. But the exit of the test phases on an agile project is still the same as a waterfall project. Performance testing of functionality will not be considered complete until after the functionality is correct.

13.3   Types of Testing

The types of testing conducted on an agile project are pretty much the same as a waterfall project. A major difference is the focus of effort and when each testing phase is conducted. Agile projects focus heavily on unit and functional testing, therefore producing high-quality code for the later phases of testing. The result is that later phases of testing are not finding defects that could have been found earlier and can focus on the areas they are trying to test. This is a common problem for waterfall projects where the focus of later testing phases is on finding defects that could have been detected earlier. The result is a higher cost of fixing defects, duplicated testing effort, and incorrect test focus.

Another significant difference between waterfall and agile projects is test automation. Agile projects strive to have 100% test automation for all areas of testing. Tests are integrated with continuous build systems, so when a change is made in the code, it is automatically detected, the application is built, and then all tests are executed.

Test-driven development (TDD) is an approach commonly used by agile projects. This approach means that test cases are written before the code is created. Using test-driven development makes it more likely that code and functionality will have test cases created for them. By driving development with automated tests and then eliminating duplication, any developer can write reliable, bug-free code no matter what its level of complexity. TDD is more commonly applied to unit testing but can also work with functional, integration, user acceptance, and performance testing.

Unit Testing

Unit testing, also known as *white box testing*, involves testing each module as it is developed. Waterfall projects do not focus on this testing phase, and in most cases it is done ad hoc if at all. Agile projects put emphasis on unit testing and automating all unit tests. The automated unit tests are the foundation of an agile project and assist continuous integration and refactoring.

Unit testing should consider the following:

- Use stubs and mocks to remove the dependency on external interfaces.
- Be written by the developers who are creating the code.

- Be automated and included with the continuous development build.
- No dependencies between unit tests, so each unit test can be executed in isolation.
- Be executable by any developer on their own machine.
- Use code coverage to determine which areas of code do not have unit tests covering them.
- 100% unit tests passing before checking in a code change.
- Any test failure means build failure.

Functional Testing

Functional testing, commonly associated with system testing, is focused on testing the functionality of the application (including negative and boundary conditions). On a waterfall project, this is generally where the testing team will start its testing activities. The team members will wait until the developers have completed all the functionality and passed the unit tests before entering this phase. Agile projects break up functionality into stories, with a number of stories being developed in an iteration. Every story has a number of acceptance criteria that are usually created by the business analyst and the test analyst and can be considered to be similar to test conditions. The test analysts will take the acceptance criteria and create test cases to demonstrate how the completed code behaves in relation to the acceptance criteria. Once the story has been coded and unit tested, it is then functionally tested to determine whether it satisfies the acceptance criteria. This means that functional testing on an agile project starts when the first piece of functionality has been coded and continues throughout the project life cycle.

Functional testing should consider the following:

- Automate and include with the development continuous build. (If the tests are taking a long time to run, then it is possible to include only a select few with the development continuous build and to include all with the system integration continuous build.)
- Write the intent of the tests before the code is written. The test implementation can be completed once the code is complete.
- Have all of the functional tests passing before a story is considered complete.
- Execute the functional tests on the application when it is installed in another environment (staging or production if possible).

Any test failure means build failure.

Exploratory Testing

Exploratory testing is also known as *ad hoc testing*. Waterfall projects do not include this type of testing in their strategy, but most testers will practice this to some degree. This is a critical phase of testing for an agile project because it is used to check the coverage of the automated tests and get general feedback on the quality of the application. It is a structured way for testers and business analysts to operate and explore the system to find defects. If exploratory testing finds a significant amount of defects in an area of functionality, then the existing automated test cases for that area are reviewed.

Exploratory testing should consider the following:

- Execute in the system integration environment.
- Capture exploratory testing activities at a high level (possibly in a wiki).
- Use an automated setup to reduce setup time.
- Include destructive testing as part of exploratory testing.

Integration Testing

Integration testing is about integrating the separate parts of the application that will be needed when the application is put into production. A waterfall project will include integrating separate modules of the application as well as applications that are not part of the project but required by the application being developed. For an agile project, the integration of separate modules of the application is covered by the continuous builds; therefore, the focus of integration testing is on external interfaces that are not being developed as part of the project.

Integration testing should consider the following:

- Consider functionality not being developed for the current iteration when performing integration testing.
- Create integration tests to target particular integration points to assist in debugging the code, even if the functional tests will provoke the integration points.
- Automate integration tests, and include them in the system integration continuous build.

Any test failure means build failure.

Data Validation

Data validation needs to be conducted if the project requires existing data to be migrated. Data validation will ensure that existing data has been migrated to the new schema correctly, new data has been added, and redundant data has been removed. Waterfall projects and agile projects approach this type of testing the same way with the only exception being that an agile project will automate the testing as much as possible.

Data validation should consider the following:

- Execute in the system integration environment, staging environment, and production environment.
- Automate as much as possible.
- Include tests in the system integration continuous build.

Any test failure means build failure.

User Acceptance Testing (UAT)

UAT focuses on complete business processes, ensuring that the application fits in with the way business works and satisfies business needs. It will also look at the usability of the application for a customer, consumer, administrator, and other user. In a waterfall project, this stage will usually be finding bugs that should have been found in the earlier stages of the testing cycle. Often, this type of testing is used by business to verify the quality of the application that has been delivered by the development team. Agile projects are able to focus UAT on ensuring the application meets business needs because the quality of the code is higher when entering this phase of testing. Because business are involved in the earlier phases of testing in an agile project, they have more confidence in what is being delivered.

UAT should consider the following:

- Do a manual pass first, and then automate when it is verified that the system behaves as it should.
- Include automated tests into the system integration continuous build.
- Get the end users of the application to conduct the manual run-through, but have it coordinated by a project tester.
- Conduct UAT on the staging environment for sign-off.
- Conduct UAT whenever a business process has been completed or major UI component is completed.

Any test failure means build failure.

Performance Testing

Performance testing covers a lot of areas but can generally be broken into three parts:

- *Capacity testing*: Checks the capacity, in isolation, of core functional components. For example, how many concurrent users can perform a search at the same time, how many searches can be performed per second, and so on? Capacity testing is used to gauge the extreme limits of a system and also to assist capacity planning and scalability.
- *Load testing*: Focuses on how a system performs when load is applied. The load should mirror the expected traffic mix the system will experience.
- *Stress testing*: Concerned with how the system behaves under stress. A soak test is a common stress-testing technique; it is putting the system under load for a sustained period of time to shake out long-term issues, such as memory leaks or resource leaks. Stress testing also covers failover and recovery, such as the failing of a server in a cluster while the system is under load to check that it fails correctly and recovers.

Waterfall projects will leave performance testing until the end of the project, once the application has been "completely" developed and been through unit and functional testing. An agile project will conduct performance tests as soon as possible.

Performance testing should consider the following:

- Place some performance metrics in the functional tests, such as seeing how long a test takes to run the first time and then comparing the percentage change (increase is bad, decrease is good) in time for each subsequent run.
- Include some performance tests in the system integration continuous build.
- Conduct performance tests whenever a business process, significant functionality, or interface has been completed.
- Only sign off on performance tests once run in the staging environment.

Any test failure means build failure.

Nonfunctional Testing

Nonfunctional testing covers a lot of different areas, and performance testing will usually fall into this. However, performance testing is an important part of an enterprise solution and needs different resource and skill sets, so it has been separated as a different test phase. Some common areas covered by nonfunctional testing include operational (including monitoring, logging, audit/history), reliability (including failover, single component, complete failure, interface failure), and security. Both waterfall and agile projects struggle with this testing phase, and there is little difference in the approach.

Nonfunctional testing should consider the following:

- Nonfunctional requirements are usually not captured or, if captured, are not easily measurable (for example, 99.9% uptime).
- Automate nonfunctional requirements as much as possible and include in the system integration testing environment.
- Involve the people who will be monitoring and supporting the production environment in the test case definition.
- Nonfunctional testing, or monitoring, continues once the application is in production.

Regression Testing

For waterfall projects, this is one of the most expensive testing phases, in time and money. If defects are found late in the project cycle, for example, in the UAT phase, then a new build of the application will require all unit tests, functional tests, and UAT tests to be rerun.

Because most waterfall projects don't have automated tests, this makes regression testing expensive. Agile projects embrace regression testing with continuous builds and automated tests, making regression testing occur for every build.

Regression testing should consider the following:

- Run manual tests at the end of each iteration (for a large set, rotate them so they are run every three to four iterations) to provide early feedback.

Production Verification

Production verification looks at the application when it is in the production environment. The testing checks that everything is installed properly and the system is operational before making it available to users. However, there may also be some testing that cannot be completely done until in the production system, and this testing will be conducted as soon as possible. There is no difference between the waterfall approach and agile approach to production verification.

Production verification should consider the following:

- Get end users to execute the production verification tests.
- Run as many automated regression tests from early test phases as possible on the production system prior to go-live.

Testing phases on a waterfall and agile project are similar, but there is a difference in the emphasis of each and when they occur. An agile project will create a lot of automated tests and use continuous integration to reduce the impact of regression testing on the project. On a waterfall project, it is common to perform testing from an earlier phase in a later phase (that is, functional testing during UAT) while the quality of the application is low. Agile projects reduce test waste, detect failures early, and increase confidence in the application being delivered.

13.4 Environments

Testing environments are used during different stages of the development process to ensure the application is working. The later in the phase that the environment is used, the more it will resemble the intended production environment. Typical testing environments include a development environment, where developers integrate their code together and can run some tests. A system integration environment is similar to the development environment but will integrate with more third-party applications and potentially a larger set of data. Staging environments mirror production as much as possible and are the last stage before production.

There is not a big difference in the environments required for an agile project vs. a waterfall project. What is different is that agile projects require all environments from the project onset and use them throughout the project life cycle. For an agile project, it is also imperative that the environment is always available and working. If it does experience problems for any reason, then it is the highest priority to get it working again. Another difference between agile and waterfall is the impact on the planning and resourcing of the environments, especially if the environments are managed by a team that is not on the project.

Development Integration Environment

A development environment is used by the developers to integrate code and produce the application being developed. A waterfall project does not consider the development environment to be of high importance; it is continually broken and is seen as being needed only when the developers have to integrate code with each other, which is generally toward the end of the project. For an agile project, the development environment is integral to the development effort and must be available before any coding is started. The environment is used to continuously integrate the code and run a suite of tests. If the environment is broken for any reason, then it is the highest priority to get it working again.

A development environment should consider the following:

- Keep the time it takes to integrate the code, build, and test to less than fifteen minutes.
- Have the development environment the same as what each developer is using. (Different hardware is OK, but software should be the same).
- Data used should be as close to production data as possible. If production data is too big to include, then a cut-down copy can be used. The data should be refreshed from production at the start of each release cycle.
- The management of the environment should be the responsibility of the project team.
- Deployment to this environment will likely occur on an hourly basis.
- Automate deployment into this environment.

System Integration Environment

A system integration environment is used to integrate the application being developed with other applications that it interacts with. For a waterfall project, this environment (if one exists) is used only toward the end of the project and is likely to be shared between projects. An agile project requires this environment to be available from the day that coding is started. The application is deployed to this environment frequently and then functional, integration, usability, and exploratory tests are executed. Demonstrations of the application (showcases) will occur from this environment.

A system integration environment should consider the following:

- Integration points should be replaced with real external applications. The external applications should be test environments and not production versions.
- Replicate the architecture of the production environment.
- Data used in this environment should be a replication of the production environment and refreshed at the start of each release cycle.
- Have a system integration continuous build that runs a complete suite of tests in this environment.
- The management of the environment should be the responsibility of the project team.
- Builds are likely to be deployed into this environment on a daily basis.
- Automate the deployment of the application into this environment.

Staging Environment

Staging environments exist to verify that the application will deploy and function in production. To this end, the staging environment is a replication of the production environment, including network configuration, routers, switches, and computer capacity. On a waterfall project, this environment will generally need to be "booked" and will have a plan of how many deployments will be needed and when they will occur. An agile project does not rely on this environment as much as it does the development and integration environments; however, it still requires frequent access with multiple deployments over the project life cycle.

A staging environment should consider the following:

- Data used should be a copy of production data and refreshed before each deployment of the application.
- Use it for sign-off of UAT, performance testing, and nonfunctional testing (stability, reliability, and so on).
- Builds are likely to be deployed into this environment on an iteration basis, such as every two weeks.
- The management of the environment should be by the same people who manage the production environment. This will give them early exposure to the application and knowledge transfer.
- Automate the deployment of the application into this environment.

Production Environment

The production environment is where the application runs when live. Production verification testing is conducted in this environment, as is gathering metrics to determine the effectiveness of the testing effort. It is similar for waterfall and agile projects. For an agile project, the release process would be automated as much as possible to allow for frequent releases into production.

A production environment should consider the following:

- Executing a suite of automated regression tests in the production environment before go-live (or just after go-live).
- Have metrics available that will help determine how effective the testing effort was, such as the severity and number of issues raised by users in the first three to six months.

Having an environment available when required is critical to any project timeline. A waterfall project will try to stick to a rigid plan, making it easy to schedule environment usage. Agile projects are more fluid. Enough functionality may be built to warrant going into a staging environment, or the business may decide to move to production early. To assist agile projects, a system integration environment should be made available with processes in place to allow for rapid deployment through staging and then into production environments.

13.5 Issue Management

Issues encompass defects (bugs) and change requests. Waterfall projects have a very strict defect and change request management, whereas agile projects are not as strict on change management as agile is about embracing change. If change is required, a new story (or stories) is created and put onto the backlog. Highest-priority stories will be assigned to the next iteration.

Defect management is still applicable to an agile project. As defects are found on a story in development, informal communication (over the shoulder) is used to communicate these defects to the developers, and the defect is addressed immediately. If a defect is found that is not for a story that is currently in the iteration or is seen as a minor defect on a story being developed, it is raised in a defect-tracking tool. The defect is then treated like a story; that is, a story card is created, prioritized by the customer, and put into the story backlog. A team needs to balance troubleshooting the defect to provide enough information for it to be understood and prioritized without spending too much time on a defect that may not be a high priority for the customer to get resolved.

Defect content (description, component, severity, and so on) is the same for an agile project and a waterfall project, except there is one extra field that should be captured for an agile project, and that is business value, in dollar terms if possible. This is the business value that would be realized if the defect were resolved. Having a business value associated with a defect makes it easier for the customer to decide whether the defect is more valuable and therefore higher priority than new functionality.

13.6 Tools

All projects will use some tools to some degree. Waterfall projects will use tools to help enforce the process as well as improve efficiency, which can sometimes cause conflicts. Agile projects will use tools to help improve efficiency, not to enforce a process. For an agile project, all tests should be able to be run by any team member in their own environment, which means that the tools used to automate the test cases have to be available to all team members. Because of this, open source products are usually used on an agile project, which means that the skills to use these tools are different. Open source tools are not documented or supported as well as commercial tools, and therefore people using them need to be proficient with coding. Pairing a developer with a person who is not a strong programmer is a good way to increase that person's skills. It is possible to use commercial tools on an agile project, but the majority of the commercial tools are not developed with the agile process in mind and therefore do not fit into it easily. In particular, continuous integration can require a lot of code to get a commercial tool to work.

For testing purposes, a project should consider tools for the following tasks:

- Continuous integration tool (for example, CruiseControl, Tinderbox)
- Unit testing (for example, JUnit, NUnit)
- Code coverage (for example, Clover, PureCoverage)
- Functional testing (for example, HttpUnit, Selenium, Quick Test Professional)

- User acceptance testing (for example, Fitness, Quick Test Professional)
- Performance testing (for example, JMeter, LoadRunner)
- Issue tracking (for example, Bugzilla, JIRA)
- Test management (for example, Quality Center)

13.7 Reports and Metrics

Metrics are gathered to determine the quality of the software and measure the testing effort. Some testing metrics for a waterfall project rely on all test cases to be created prior to the test effort and testing to occur only once the application is finished. Then metrics such as how many defects found per test case executed and test cases executed per day can be collected and used to determine whether the application is ready for release. On agile projects, the test cases are created and executed when functionality is complete, which means the metrics used for waterfall testing cannot be applied.

Returning to the reason for gathering metrics, to determine the quality of the application and measure the testing effort, you can look at the following areas:

- Measure the testing effort using code coverage; this is particularly useful for unit tests.
- The number of defects found during exploratory testing will show how effective the unit and functional testing efforts are.
- Defects found during UAT indicate that the earlier testing is not as sufficient as UAT and should focus on business process and not software bugs. If UAT is finding a lot of issues that are functional rather than software bugs, this indicates a lack of understanding in the stories or changing requirements.
- The number of defects found after the story has been completed is a good measure of software quality. This is the number of defects (software bugs, not functional changes) found in integration, nonfunctional, performance, and UAT tests.
- Rate of reopened defects. If defects are reopened frequently, it indicates that the quality of the software is low.

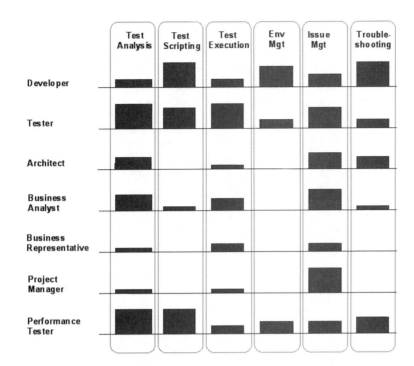

Figure 13.2: TESTING ROLES FOR DIFFERENT TEAM MEMBERS

13.8 Testing Roles

Testing roles do not equate to a single resource. A single resource may perform all the testing roles, or each role may be performed by separate people. The roles outlined are those that are needed to ensure the testing effort of a project is successful. A good tester will have elements of all these roles. The roles are the same for an agile project as they are for a waterfall project; the difference is who performs the roles. For an agile project, all team members will perform some testing roles. In Figure 13.2, you'll see an example of the roles that each team member on an agile project will take on. This is not prescriptive; each team is different, but this is seen as a good mix.

Test Analysis

Test analysis looks at the requirements, architecture, code, or other artifacts to determine what should be tested and where testing should be focused.

On a waterfall project there would normally be a senior resource (or resources) who will perform this role. They examine relevant documents (requirements, design, architecture), create test plans, create high-level test case descriptions, and then hand off everything to a junior person to fill in the detailed test scripts. Agile projects encourage all team members to perform this role. Developers will focus on the analysis of the code and design to create unit tests, and they may also assist the business analyst or testers when creating functional tests and will be involved in analysis for nonfunctional and performance tests. The business analyst and testers work closely to create functional tests, create user acceptance tests, and perform exploratory testing. Customers/end users will be engaged for the user acceptance tests.

Test Scripting

A scripting role is one that creates the detailed test scripts. These could be manual or automated. A scripter on a waterfall project will normally be a junior person who uses the test plans and test case descriptions to create the detailed, step-by-step manual instructions. Automated scripting is performed by a more senior person, and developers may be involved in scripting unit test cases. An agile project will use developers a lot for test scripting, mainly because the test scripts are automated.

Test Execution

This role exists for both manual and automated tests; however, for automated tests, the role is performed by a computer. A test executor will execute the detailed test scripts and determine whether the test passes or fails. This role in a waterfall project will normally be conducted by testers. For an agile project, all team members are encouraged to perform this role, in particular testers, business analysts, and the customer.

Environment Management

This role manages the testing environments, including the environment that the application runs on as well as the infrastructure required to support automated testing. They will also look after data used for testing and external interfaces. This role is similar in both waterfall and agile projects.

Issue Management

Issues are raised and need to be followed up on. This role helps triage issues to ensure that they are correctly created, including the severity, priority, component, and so on. Issue lifecycle and tool support is also part of this role. This role is very similar in waterfall and agile projects.

Troubleshooting

This role troubleshoots issues as they are raised to determine whether they are software defects. For software defects, they will look at what the cause is and possible solutions and workarounds. This role is similar in waterfall and agile projects.

Agile teams focus on ensuring that the roles are adequately performed with less focus on who is doing them and who is responsible for them. There is little delineation between testers and other team members, with more focus on making sure that the team delivers. As a team, it is important that the software being produced is of high quality, and each team member contributes in any way they can to achieve this goal. On an agile team, testers can expect to get support from all team members and in return assist others in improving their testing skills. This approach ensures everybody on the team is committed to delivering a quality application.

13.9 References

Test-Driven Development: By Example by Kent Beck (Addison-Wesley Professional, 2002)

"Exploratory Testing Explained v.1.3 4/16/03," copyright 2002–2003 by James Bach, http://www.James@satisfice.com

Chapter 14

Pragmatic Performance Testing

by James Bull, QA Consultant

Software that performs poorly will annoy people and hinder organizations rather than make their lives easier. It will, regardless of the level of functionality delivered, have a strong negative impact on the perceived quality of the software. People who have had a bad experience with software from your company won't wait to see whether you can do better next time. They will vote with their wallets and take their money elsewhere.

Given the choice between a fast, reliable system that scales well and a system that does not, the decision is obvious. When we talk about performance testing, we generally use it to encompass scalability and reliability as well as performance because they are often done at the same time using the same tools. In this essay, I'll talk about how to ensure that the finished product has these properties that I will often refer to collectively as *performance*.

14.1 What Is Performance Testing?

At this point, we are probably all in agreement that the previously mentioned software attributes are not just a good thing but are worth paying money for. The question now is, where does performance testing fit into all this? How does that help us with our goal of writing software with an appropriate level of performance?

Performance testing should encompass all the activities necessary to make sure that the product released has satisfactory performance. There are four key elements: requirements, product performance data, communication, and process.

If any of these elements are missing, then performance testing will be significantly less effective. If the only activity undertaken is testing, you aren't really in a much better position, because it is not known how fast it is supposed to go. For this reason, you need to do some requirements gathering too. If the results are not communicated, then nobody knows that there is a problem, so no action can be taken. Even when we have established the requirements, tested the product, and communicated the results, we are still not finished. If there is no room in the plan for performance bug fixing or no established process by which the work needed gets planned based on the communicated results, then you have minimal impact on the software that actually gets shipped. In this final case, you have spent a significant amount of money ensuring you are very well informed about the exact extent of your failure or success with regard to performance.

What we want is not just to be well informed but to allow the information gained to have an effect on the software that is being written, thus ensuring we meet or, at worst, get closer to meeting the desired level of performance. I'll discuss each of these four elements in detail.

14.2 Requirements Gathering

Requirements gathering is often undervalued and overlooked. I'll try to explain what we are measuring, how we know what we want, and how to come up with numbers that are actually going to be helpful and not counterproductive.

What Are We Measuring?

The key measurements for performance are maximum throughput and response time at a given level of throughput. It is good to measure response times at a number of different throughput volumes to see how system load affects the response time. If you have stringent response time targets, then maybe the throughput it can achieve while maintaining those targets will be significantly lower than the maximum. You want to find the throughput at which response times are acceptable and the response times you get when running at the desired throughput.

The key measurements for scalability are how the initial performance measurements vary as the size of the data set and the number of users or the hardware the system is running on changes.

The key measurements for reliability are whether the system continues to function correctly when under an abnormally high load and whether the system continues to function correctly when run for a long time.

How Do You Set a Figure?

To know what throughput the system will need to achieve, you need to know how many users there will be on the system and what their pattern of usage is going to be. How often does a user perform a given function, and how quickly does it need to be completed?

This information should be available from somebody in the business. You should prepare them for the fact that this information will be needed on a regular basis and then establish a process that will allow this information to be gathered with a minimum of fuss.

You want to reach a state where you can reliably obtain the information you need and have a process whereby you can arrive at the figures that are necessary to support the business at that particular moment in time. If you don't calculate these numbers regularly, you can end up working toward targets that have been rendered irrelevant.

Once you have determined the throughput that is currently required, you can start to think about the response times. When considering the UI, it is easy to fall into the trap of thinking that because you want the user interface to respond in a fraction of a second, the function it is executing must also be completed in this time. The UI should respond immediately with a display informing the user that their request is being processed. The rest of the application that does not depend on the function being executed should still be available.

Response time targets should be primarily for the user interface and should be low. They should not carry the expectation that any given function should complete within that time.

Just in case that isn't clear, the following is a quick example.

How Does This Fit in with the Normal Software Development Process?

Ideally, the meetings to determine the performance requirements for the current week's work should include the project manager, the performance stakeholder, a senior developer, and the performance tester. The developer is required in order to point out whether any of the requirements being looked at are obviously not going to be met or are unreasonable. The performance stakeholder is there to provide information and knowledge about the business to help determine the requirements. The project manager needs to know what is being decided and provide some direction, and the performance tester obviously needs to be present so they know what they are testing against.

Next you need to decide who you are going to have these discussions with. It is very important that there is a point of contact within the business who will share the responsibility for determining performance requirements. This ensures that the customer knows what they want and that the developers know what they want too. The requirements that we come up with should not be regarded as inviolable. As with all requirements, they should be a starting point for dialogue with the customer about what is achievable.

Once the requirements have been set, you can agree on how you will show that these requirements have been met and then estimate and plan the work to develop these tests as you would with any other piece of work.

Don't the Developers Also Have Requirements from the Performance Testing?

The requirements the developers have will vary, but the driver for them is that if a certain piece of code needs rework, then they will need additional information about what was happening at the time. This could vary from output from a code profiler to thread dumps or even just some additional logging. They may want to know how busy the database was compared to the application server or how busy the network was during times of peak load.

It is probably not worth trying to answer all these questions up front because this would represent a significant amount of work. What you can do, though, is where there is some code that needs rework, you can work out what information the developers need in order to effectively fix the problem and then go through this with the client and add it to the list of tasks you need to do. You can at this time consider whether it would be easy to do this for all tests from now on or whether this is going to be a once-off exercise for this particular incident.

When the developers' requirements are brought up in the requirements meeting in this way, everyone is aware of them. They can be taken into account when prioritizing and planning the work later. The end result will be that the performance testing that is done is able to satisfy both parties' requirements. It will give the customer confidence in the software as it is being developed. And it will help the developers track down and eliminate any issues that occur.

What If You Can't Find a Stakeholder for Performance Requirements?

If you can't find a stakeholder for performance requirements, then there are several risks. The first is that you will create software that is inappropriate for the business, and the project will fail. The second is that the customer will disagree about whether the software is appropriate regardless of the actual suitability of the product because they think they have not been consulted. The third risk is that you might create tension in the team as you push for the development team to do work that they see as unnecessary because it has not come from the customer. This can happen whether your concerns are valid or not and can result in necessary work not getting done or, conversely, time being wasted doing work that is not necessary.

What Happens If the Customer Isn't Very Technical and Wants Something We Believe Is Impossible?

There is a risk that the customer might want a level of performance from the product that is either impossible or uneconomic to achieve. You want to prevent this from happening by directing the conversation toward what the business actually requires by asking some pertinent questions.

Some questions to consider when it comes to throughput are, how many transactions are processed every business day? How are these transactions distributed? Do they come in evenly spread, or are there peaks and troughs? Is there a rush every Friday afternoon, or is there no particular pattern to when the peaks occur?

Questions to consider when it comes to response time are, how will the response time of the user interface affect the amount of work that can be done with the system? Can the interface be decoupled from the actual action being performed? For example, you might have a scenario where a user inputs some data that is then subject to some lengthy data processing. The user does not want to wait for the data processing to finish before they enter their next piece of data, so rather than expect the data processing to complete in a second, decouple the interface from the processing and allow the system to work on this data in the background while allowing the user to continue entering data using the interface.

In this way, we keep both parties focused on the level of performance that will actually help the business, and we are able to differentiate between what is actively needed and what is simply nice to have. It might turn out that what is genuinely needed is not possible given the current constraints on the project or that it will be very expensive. In this case, the client can decide whether to proceed at an earlier stage than would otherwise have been possible if this requirements analysis were not done.

The bad thing about the customer wanting something they can't have is that they will be disappointed with the final system even though it may perform well enough to satisfy their business needs. These discussions will have a dual function. They will bring to light the actual requirements the business has while at the same time making the client aware of what it is they require. This will lead to the client being satisfied with the system if it does what they need. They are much less likely to have their expectations confounded, and if they are disappointed, then it is likely to be with good reason.

Why Not Get the Business Analysts to Gather These Requirements As Well?

It is not necessary to have a business analyst present for a couple of reasons. The first is that the functional requirements gathering will already have been done. The second is that even if a business analyst were present, this would not remove the need for a developer to be there because they are need to articulate the requirements they have for investigating performance problems while also being there to flag whether any of the things that are required are likely to cause difficulties or require a different approach. The performance tester should be able to drive the conversation by asking questions similar to the previous ones. They can also say how easy or difficult it will be to test each function. In this case, the business analyst's time would be better spent elsewhere.

Summary

The purpose of requirements gathering is to be well informed about how well the product needs to perform in order to be able to support the business goals. The reason for involving the customer is that they are the ones with the most knowledge of their own business. This helps ensure that the requirements you gather are accurate. It also has the benefit of making the customer explicitly aware of what their requirements in this area are, and so it manages their expectations of the final system.

14.3 Running the Tests

I'll talk briefly now about the sort of tests you want to run and when you want to run them.

What Tests Are You Running Again?

You want a test for all frequently performed user actions. These tests should record throughput, error rate, and response time metrics. You then want to reuse these tests to create more complex ones. You want a test that runs all these tests together in a realistic distribution. This will give you sufficient information about the performance of the product.

Once you have done this, you then take the realistic test and run it with differing numbers of users and different size data sets to see how it scales. If it is possible, you also want to run the system on different numbers of machines to show how the performance changes as more hardware is added. This will give you the information you need for scalability.

Finally, you want a test that puts the system under more load than you expect so you can find the failure points. You also want a test based on the realistic test with similar distributions of users but sped up. Running this for a long period of time should tell you how reliable the system is.

When Should You Run Them?

The obvious answer is as often as possible. There is a problem with this, of course. Performance test suites by their nature tend to take a long time to run. Reliability tests particularly need to run for a long time to be useful, so there are not enough hours in the day to run a comprehensive performance test suite on every build. You want to provide rapid feedback to the developers and also test the product comprehensively.

One solution is to have a single dedicated box that runs a limited set of performance tests continuously on the latest build. It should be set to fail if the results differ markedly from the previous build. The results you get from this will not be indicative of the real-world performance but will be an early warning system that will quickly tell developers whether something they have done has caused a significant change in the way the product performs.

The full suite of tests should then be running on the full performance environment as often as it can. This might be several times a day, or if access to the environment is limited, then running them overnight is a good compromise.

The reliability test obviously has to take a long time, and often it has to be run on the same environment as everything else. This means it cannot be done during the week, so running it over the weekend every week is about as good as you can hope to get without having a separate environment dedicated to reliability testing.

Where Should You Run Them?

If at all possible, you should try to get hold of a system that mimics the production system. If this is not possible because the production system is too large, then you need to build an environment that mimics a slice of the production environment and express the absolute requirements in terms of a figure per server.

If it is not possible to get access to a dedicated performance testing environment, then things start to get a little tricky. If you have to share with the functional testing team, then running the performance suite overnight is one option. In this case, it is wise to have separate databases for the performance and functional tests and a script to swap the program under test between them. This means that the two conflicting uses of the system will not interfere with each other. This of course assumes that it is possible to run the application under test on a desktop machine and develop the performance tests on that.

One issue to be careful of when running at night is that the network conditions will be different from those during the day. The network may be less busy because people are not in work, but there is also the possibility that backups or other overnight batch processes will have a significant effect on the network traffic. A burst of network activity during a performance test may well affect the results, and if both the performance tests and the job that causes the traffic are scheduled to start at the same time, then there could be a consistent effect on the results that you won't see unless you run the test at a different time. Arranging to run the test suite once during a normal working day will let you know whether there are significant differences in your test results because of time differences. If there is a big difference, then you can either try to simulate the average network traffic you would get during a normal day or see whether the difference between running at the two times is consistent and just take that into account when looking at the results.

In my experience where there is significant contention for a test environment, it is necessary to be very organized with regard to whom uses the system, at what time, and running against which database. It is also the case that sometimes a test will fail on the test environment yet pass on the local machine. This will require the environment to be switched across to the performance database and the rest of QA not to use the system until the issue is resolved. Because of these difficulties and the fact that sharing an environment significantly limits how often you run your tests, it is worth trying to organize a separate environment for running these tests if at all possible, even if this means the environment you run the tests on most often is not production-like.

If you end up with a situation where you must choose between a non-production-like environment or limited time on a production-like one, then take both. The exclusive environment allows you to have unhindered access to develop and run tests on a regular basis. This could then be included in the continuous integration system. The production-like environment allows you to compare the results you get on that system to the results you get on the nonproduction system you run on more regularly. This will give you an idea of how the results you get are likely to relate to the ultimate performance of the system.

How Do You Relate Test Results on a Smaller Test Rig to Production?

One problem that often occurs is that the environment you have is not the same as the production one. It is important to realize that having a test system with no similarities at all to production makes it almost impossible to judge how the system will perform on different hardware. So when you necessarily have to have a smaller environment, what can you do? Here I am going to go into greater detail about what I mean by the representative slice of the system.

Consider the example of a large-volume web application. The basic architecture of the system might be several application servers, a number of web servers, and some database servers. If in the production system there are a number of database servers (very big boxes), two times the number of application servers per database server (big boxes), and four web servers per application server (little boxes), then you might consider the following approach. Buy one database server half as powerful as a production one. Buy one application server that is the same specification as one of the ones in production, and buy one web server.

You then have an application server/database combination where the specification of the machines relative to each other is the same but should be about half the speed. You also have an inadequate web server capacity.

You can find out what the performance of the application is by hitting the application servers directly. This will give you a figure for what each application server can achieve. You then test through the single web server you have, which in this scenario should show the web server to be a bottleneck. This will allow you to get a per-server figure for the web server that is not held back by the rest of the system. You should be able to use this to tell whether the ratio of different types of machines mooted for the production system is correct and come up with an estimate of the performance of the production system that you have a certain degree of confidence in.

One thing to remember is that given that every web request will be served only from a single application server/database combination as the number of machines increases, only the throughput will increase as a direct result of this. The response time will improve only as a result of increases in the amount of CPU power or memory available per machine, assuming the level of load the system is subjected to remains the same. A faster CPU will process more requests more quickly, while more memory allows more items to be cached.

This does of course assume that the machines remain the same, that the CPUs are all from the same manufacturer, that they are all running the same version of the same OS, and that they are running the same database/webserver/appserver combination.

Do bear in mind that the further the system is from production in terms of specification of machines, software used, and so on, the less confidence you should have in any estimate you make of the performance of the final system. In the previous example, you could put together a test environment for a fraction of the cost of the full production kit, and you could have some confidence that the numbers projected for the final system would not be too far off. If you had machines with wildly different specifications that used MySQL instead of Oracle or WebSphere instead of JBoss, then although you could still measure performance changes, any projection would be of dubious value.

What Size Database Is Appropriate for Performance Testing?

When running performance tests, it is important to note that the size of a database can have a very large impact on the time it takes to retrieve rows from a table. If a table is not correctly indexed, then the problem may not be apparent with a small data set; however, if your production data has more than a few thousand rows, then the performance will degrade significantly.

You should have a chat with the performance stakeholder about getting hold of a copy of the production database so you can test the code against that. When doing this, it is important that you are aware of data protection issues and that the database you use has been suitably cleaned to remove or change personal information.

You should also discuss with the performance stakeholder how the volume of data is stored is likely to change. Will it remain roughly constant, or is it likely to grow? If it's going to grow, is it going to grow slowly or quickly? Knowing this will help you decide whether it is appropriate to test with a database significantly larger than the current one.

The best way to get a larger database is to use your stability tests to create a new database. As part of your stability test, you should be creating new users and new transactions, and if the system successfully runs all weekend, then you should have a sizable data set you can use in the future.

How Do You Deal with Third-Party Interfaces?

When a system has many third-party interfaces, it is a good idea not to hit these systems directly. There are two reasons for this. The first is that the third parties will probably not be pleased to be part of your performance tests, and the second is that even where they do provide a test environment, relying on a third party that you have no control over will make your tests less reliable.

The best thing to do is to perform a test to find out how quickly this system responds on average and then write a mock or stub that simply waits this long before returning a fixed response. You could simply have it return a response immediately, but then you would be losing a certain amount of realism from your scenario because the application server could potentially be working its way through database connections or network connections faster than it otherwise would, which could make a difference to the final results.

How Many Different Test Cases Do You Need?

This is quite an important question because using the wrong amount of data will skew the results badly whether you use too much or too little. If you use a too few test cases, all the relevant bits of information will become cached, and your results will show the system to be quicker than it actually is. If you use too many different test cases, then you will find that you burst the cache, and the system will appear to be slower than it will actually be in normal operation.

To use the correct number of test cases, you will need to discuss the expected usage of the system with the performance stakeholder and if possible get the logs of usage for the existing system. For example, if you are retrieving customer information inside an application, then obviously the number of customers whose information you retrieve should be comparable to the number of unique customers retrieved during normal operation. If 5% of the records in the system are retrieved in any given day, then your test cases should cover this number of customers.

Why Take Several Different Measurements for Response Time and Throughput?

In general, as you begin to increase load from idle, the response time of the system is unlikely to degrade. As load continues to increase, there will come a point where the total number of transactions processed per unit time continues to increase (that is, throughput goes up), but this comes at the expense of response time, which will also begin to rise. As the server reaches its maximum capacity, throughput initially remains constant while response times begin to increase significantly before finally the throughput itself collapses because the machine is just unable to keep up with the volume of work it is being asked to do. At this point, response times will shoot up, and the whole system will grind to a halt.

You are interested in several pieces of information. The first thing you want to know is the point at which the maximum throughput of the system occurs. Other interesting pieces of information are the load level at which response times meet their targets, the best achievable response time, and the response times at 80% and 90% of the previously measured maximum throughput.

This allows you to limit the number of connections the application server will accept per machine to keep the performance characteristics of the system within the bounds agreed on during the requirements gathering. You will notice that the variability of response times will increase dramatically as you approach maximum load and are significantly less variable at 80% or even 90% capacity. This is worth bearing in mind if you have to guarantee a certain level of performance.

Is It Necessary to Test Every Function in the System?

It is rarely feasible to test every single piece of functionality in the system. What is important, though, is to make sure you hit the functions that are used most often. To do this, you need to identify the major ways the system is used and create different tests for each scenario.

For example, in an online shopping site the major usage modes might be browsing and buying. Not everyone who comes to buy an item will do so after extensive browsing, and not everyone will browse for a long time. What you need to do is create one script for browsing and one for buying. The information you need to make these scripts realistic is the average number of items a browser browses, the number of items on the average order, and the total percentage of all items that get browsed by all users on the site over the course of a typical day.

Summary

Many questions can arise in the course of performance testing. What should you measure? How often? How many scripts? How much data? The main thing to remember is that your regular chats to the performance stakeholder should be the forum in which questions like these are aired and where needed information can be gathered. You should also make time to talk to the project manager and the performance stakeholder if you think the way things are going are having a significant impact on the efficacy of these tests.

14.4 Communication

Communicating the results is important. The question then is, what exactly is it that we are communicating? Communicating the results is about more than just reporting raw numbers. If you do this, you are requiring everybody on the team to spend time analyzing the results when they have other things to do. It makes it easier for everyone if the results are subject to some basic analysis and interpretation and a summary is presented.

Therefore, you need to interpret the results with respect to the requirements that have been agreed on and with respect to the current level of performance. First, you want to report on how close the performance is to the target, either faster or slower. Second, you want to report whether the performance of an aspect of the product changes significantly. You would want this to be widely known whether or not it causes you to miss performance targets. It could be the case that a large piece of additional functionality has gone in, which unavoidably affects the performance of the product, in which case there might be little that could be done. It might, however, be something as simple as a missing index on the database, which would be easy to fix.

Who Needs to Know?

Three sets of people need to have the results communicated to them: the developers, the project manager, and the client. The developers and the project manager need to know as soon as the tests are run so that the team can deal with any issues appropriately as soon as they occur. You don't necessarily want to be bothering the client every day with small problems, though; otherwise, they will be less inclined to listen when you have something important to tell them. You don't want to neglect it, however, so having a scheduled meeting once a week when you can go through the results is probably a good idea.

It's also worth considering that different people are interested in different information. It might be that clients or project managers want to see a higher-level view of the information, while the developers are more interested in the raw data, how many responses are within a given period, and so on. If you can provide the right information to the right people, then it makes the job of communicating the status of the product a lot easier.

So, You Just Need to Create a Report, Right?

Not quite. The problem with just creating a report and sending it round is that it means the majority of people won't read it, so the information you want to convey will be lost. Any report you create is just a tool to help you to get your message across; it doesn't mean you can stop at that point.

It is useful to have a website you can direct people to that contains the latest performance test results. Then when you go over to someone's desk to tell them about the results, you can bring up the web page and take them through what you have found. Unfortunately, test reports do not make riveting reading for the majority of people, and the only way you can be sure you have got your message across is to go to their desk or pick up the phone and go through the report with them.

Summary

You are aiming to be in a situation where, because your requirements are well known, you do not have to ask the client every time a test result comes in whether it is acceptable. When you meet on a weekly basis to go through the current status of the project, you want to be able to point out any anomalies or abnormalities in the test results and explain them. If the software is particularly bad in a particular area but it has been judged not to be a serious issue, then you should be able to tell them why it is slower and that the project manager did not think it was a high priority and give them the reason why. If they disagree with the decision, then it is time for the project manager and the customer to sit down and have a discussion about the current situation.

14.5 Process

Performance testing is often left until the end of a project, but this has a significant effect on how effective it can be. The most important thing about doing performance testing is to do it regularly. If you leave it until the last few weeks of a project, then you will have a lot of work to do in a small timeframe. You will spend most of your time writing scripts and getting some numbers out of the product. You will then be in a situation where it is known roughly how fast the system is, but there is little idea whether this is good enough, and there is no time to make any changes that might be required.

Performance testing should start as the first piece of code is being developed. Although there may not yet be anything you can test, there are still lots of things you can do. You can talk to the developers about the technology they will be using, evaluate suitable tools, and find one that provides the functionality you will need to test this product. You can also identify a performance stakeholder and begin the requirements-gathering process with them.

So, How Do You Link It All Together?

From this point onward, you can start to get into a cycle. At the beginning of the week you meet with the performance stakeholder for the first time. This meeting is to discuss requirements for the functions currently being implemented. It is also a place where you can describe the tests you plan to create and how that would show that the requirements were satisfied. The customer can also request additional tests at this point. Throughout the rest of the week, you can be implementing tests for the most recently completed functionality, maintaining the automated tests, and checking the results. At the end of the week, you meet with the performance stakeholder again. The purpose of this second meeting is twofold. First you are showing them the tests you have written during the week. You can then discuss with the client whether these new tests actually show that the product meets the requirements you discussed earlier. The second purpose of the meeting is to go over the current results for the existing performance tests.

How Do You Make Sure You Don't Drop Behind?

As you are working to a weekly cycle, it should become apparent very quickly whether you are dropping behind. To catch up again, you can either increase the resources allocated to performance testing or reduce the amount of work that you try to do. Which of these you choose should be largely dependent on just how important the performance requirements for this project are.

One way to do this is to create a list of tasks that are required based on the tests that you and the client have decided upon. You can then go through the list of tests with the client and prioritize them. You then do as many as you can in a week and then move on. If this approach results in very spotty test coverage, then it may be that more effort is required for performance testing. You will probably find, however, that by dropping the most difficult and lowest-priority tests, you can develop a suite of tests that provides adequate coverage without falling behind.

How Do You Make Sure That Once an Issue Is Identified That Something Gets Done About It?

Talking to the project manager at the start of the project about how performance fixes will be dealt with is important here. You need to make sure they agree with this approach and think the requirements you are gathering are valid. You want to ensure that they are happy for you to raise performance issues as bugs and that they will be worked on as they occur so that you do not find yourself in the situation where there are a large number of known issues to address at the end of the project. There is, after all, little value in identifying whether the current performance is acceptable if you then take no action to remedy it when it becomes necessary.

14.6 Summary

The main benefit of these processes is that it ensures that you know what you need, you know what you actually have, and you ensure that you have some tests for every part of the system. This greatly increases the chance that you will be able to deal with any problems that occur. The fact that you are able to test each feature as it is developed means you have time to change it if it is necessary. The fact that you have requirements means you know whether a change is required. The fact that the requirements come from the client and are based on their business processes and volumes means that the whole team has confidence in them. This in turn means that people will be happy to spend the time needed to fix performance bugs because they know each one represents a valuable piece of work.

Bibliography

[Eva03]   Eric Evans. *Domain-Driven Design: Tackling Complexity in the Heart of Software*. Addison-Wesley Professional, Reading, MA, first edition, 2003.

[FBB+99]   Martin Fowler, Kent Beck, John Brant, William Opdyke, and Don Roberts. *Refactoring: Improving the Design of Existing Code*. Addison Wesley Longman, Reading, MA, 1999.

[GHJV95]   Erich Gamma, Richard Helm, Ralph Johnson, and John Vlissides. *Design Patterns: Elements of Reusable Object-Oriented Software*. Addison-Wesley, Reading, MA, 1995.

Index

A

Abbreviating, 67–68
Acceptance tests, 170
Agile vs. waterfall test strategy, 177
    data validation, 184
    environments, testing, 187–190
    exploratory testing, 183
    functional testing, 182
    integration testing, 183
    issue management, 190
    nonfunctional testing, 186
    performance testing, 185
    production verification, 187
    regression testing, 186
    reports and metrics for, 192
    test types, 181
    testing life cycle, 179f, 178–180
    testing roles for, 193f, 193–195
    tools for, 191–192
    unit testing, 181
    user acceptance testing, 184
Annotations
    domain, 116–117
    domain, benefits of, 117–118
    domain-driven design and, 113–114
    domain-specific metadata and, 114
    Java and .NET and, 115–116
Ant, refactoring, 135–164
    taskname attribute, 159–160
    build files, 136–137
    CI publishers and, 161
    declarations in, 143
    dependencies in, 144
    deployment code, 149–150
    descriptions vs. comments, 149
    directories, centralizing, 160
    elements and antlibs, 150–152
    elements, reusing, 154–156
    Exac vs. Apply, 161
    filtersfile, 145–146
    internal targets, 160
    invoking, 159
    library definitions and filesets, 152–153
    literal values and properties, 144–145
    location attribute, 157
    macrodef, 139–141
    move target to wrapper build file, 147–149
    name and description catalog, 137–163
    path and option scripts, moving, 157–159
    properties files, 146–147
    properties, moving outside target, 156
    runtime properties, 153–154
    target naming, 162–163
    targets, extracting, 141–142
Apache Commons project, 54
Assembly, 48
Associative arrays, tuples as, 57
Automation
    continuous integration pipeline and, 174, 175f
    deployment and, 171–173
    "Last mile" problem and, 9
    nonfunctional requirements testing and, 11–12

B

Bay, Jeff, 61–71
Bill of Rights, developers, 75
Binaries, managing, 167–168
Bottlenecks, 84
Breaking changes, 101–103
Budget burn-down, 88f, 87–89

Bug counts, 86f, 86–87
Bull, James, 197–213
Business software, *see* Last Mile
  problem; Enterprise web
  applications
Business value
  and agile processes, 13–14
  "Last mile" problem and, 6–7

C

C, 48
C++, 48
Class methods, 21–23
Classes
  collections and, 70
  entities and, 68
  instance variables, 68–69
Closures, 27–28
Cockburn, Alistair, 82
Code
  qualities for, 61
  standards for, 62
Code katas, 38
Command query separation, 22
Commit-tests, 168
Communication
  "Last mile" problem and, 8–9
  performance testing and, 210–211
  see also Iteration manager
Compiled languages, 47
Computer languages
  characteristics of, 47–48
  conflict over, 49
  Erlang, 42
  execution behavior, 46–47
  Fortran, 40
  Haskell, 41–42
  implementation models, 47
  Java, 41
  Lisp, 40–41
  paradigms, 43–44
  vs. platform, 51
  polyglot programming and, 51–60
  Ruby, 41
  SQL, 42
  type characteristics of, 44–45
  varieties of, 43–47
  see also Dynamic languages
Concurrent languages, 46
Configuration objects, 17
Consumer contracts, 106–107

Consumer-driven contracts, 93
  benefits of, 110
  breaking changes and, 101–103
  characteristics of, 108
  consumer contracts and, 106–107
  evolving a service and, 95–96
  implementation of, 109
  liabilities and, 111–112
  provider contracts and, 103–106
  schema versioning and, 96–101
  service-level agreements and, 111
  service-oriented architecture
    overview and, 93–94
Context variables, 19
Continuous integration, 12, 165–175
  acceptance tests, 170
  automation of, 174, 175f
  defined, 148
  deployment, 171–173
  end-to-end release systems, 166–167
  full lifecycle pipeline, 167–168, 171f
  practice of, 165–166
  release candidate, 168–169
  test stages, 173–174
Conversations, *see* Communication
Counter-based testing, 11
Current state of implementation, 89f,
  90f, 89–91
Customers, iteration managers and, 78
Customers, requirements gathering
  and, 201

D

Data encapsulation, 70–71
Data validation, 184
Declarations, Ant, 143
Declarative languages, 42
Decomposition, 69
Delivery quality, 86f, 86–87
Dependencies, Ant, 144
Deployment, 171–173
Design, *see* Object-oriented design;
  Domain annotations
Design vs. production environment,
  12–13
Design, code qualities for, 61
Development integration environment,
  188
Doernenburg, Erik, 113–133
Domain annotations, 113–133
  benefits of, 117–118

characteristics of, 116–117
design and, 113–114
Java and .NET and, 115–116
Leroy's Lorries case study, 119–132
  data classification in, 121–126
  domain model of, 119–120
  navigational hints for, 126–132
  transfers, 119f
  users, 121f
metadata and, 114
Domain-specific languages, *see* DSLs
Dots per line, 66–67
DSLs
  closures and, 27–28
  dynamic reception and, 36–38
  evaluation context and, 28–31
  global functions and, 18–21
  internal, 15
  lair example background, 15–18
  literal collections and, 31–36
  objects and, 21–27
  variables in, 20
Duck typing, 45
Dynamic languages
  Lisp as, 40
  method calls and, 36
  unknown methods and, 37
Dynamic reception, 36–38
Dynamic typing, 45
Dynamically typed languages, 40

E

Elements, reusing, 154–156
else, 64–65
Encapsulation, 70–71
Enterprise web applications, 177
  data validation, 184
  environments, testing, 187–190
  exploratory testing, 183
  functional testing, 182
  integration testing, 183
  issue management, 190
  nonfunctional testing, 186
  performance testing, 185
  production verification, 187
  regression testing, 186
  reports and metrics for, 192
  test types, 181
  testing life cycle, 179f, 178–180
  testing roles, 193f, 193–195
  tools for, 191–192

unit testing, 181
user acceptance testing, 184
Entities, 68
Environment variables, 145
Environments, testing, 187–190
Erlang, 42, 48
Evaluation context, 28–31
Evans, value objects, 20
Execution behavior, 46–47
Exploratory testing, 183
Expression Builder, 23–26

F

Farley, Dave, 165–175
filtersfile, 145–146
Finger chart, 77
First-class collections, 70
Ford, Neal, 51–60
Fortran, 40, 48
Fowler, Martin, 15–38
Functional languages, 40, 41, 56
Functional programming, Jaskell and, 55–58
Functional testing, 182
Functions, global, 18–21

G

George, Fred, 73, 77, 79
getters/setters properties, 70
Global functions, 18–21
  objects and, 21–27
Greenspun Form, 35
Groovy, 52–54

H

Haskell, 41–42, 48
  see also Jaskell

I

Identifiers, 20
if element, 144
if/else construct, 64–65, 143
Imperative languages, 40
Implementation models, 47
Implementing Lean Software Development: From Concept to Cash (Poppendieck & Poppendieck), 78
Indentation, 63–64
Information radiator, 90

Information radiators, 82
Instance variables, 68–69
Integrated development environments (IDEs), 48
Integration testing, 183
Interfaces, provider contracts and, 104
Interfaces, third-party, 207
Interpreted languages, 47
Issue management, 190
Iteration manager, 73–80
    customers and, 78
    iterations and, 78–79
    project environment and, 79
    vs. project manager, 75–76
    project vital signs and, 84
    role of, 73–74
    skills and responsibilities of, 74–77
    team and, 76–77

J

Jaskell, 55–58
Java, 41, 48
    annotations in, 116
    isBlank(), 54–55
    origins of, 51
    reading files in, 52
    testing, 58–60
    see also Ant; Polyglot programming
JMock, 58
JRuby, 54–55, 59

K

Katas, 38
Key, 33, 34

L

Languages, see Computer languages;
    Dynamic languages
"Last mile" problem, 5–14
    automation and, 9
    business value and, 6–7
    communication and, 8–9
    defined, 5
    design and production environment, 12–13
    nonfunctional requirements testing, 11–12
    solving, 8
    source of, 5–6
    versionless software and, 13–14

Law of Demeter, 66–67
Lazy languages, 41, 46
Legacy systems
    "Last mile" problem and, 7
    automation and, 10
    versionless software and, 14
Lentz, Tiffany, 73–80
Leroy's Lorries case study, 119–132
    data classification in, 121–126
    domain model of, 119–120
    navigation in, 126–132
    transfers, 119f
    users, 121f
Liabilities, consumer-driven contracts and, 111–112
Lisp, 40–41, 48
    vs. Ruby, 15
Lists, 33–35
Literal collections (maps and lists), 31–36
Literal hash, 32
Literal values and properties, 144–145

M

Macrodefs, 139–141
Maps, 32
Meetings, iteration managers and, 78–79
Meetings, performance testing and, 200
Metadata
    .NET and, 115
    domain-specific, 114
Method chaining, 21–23
    vs. parameters, 26
Method missing, 37
Methods
    class, 21–23
    indentation of, 63–64
    poorly hung, 54
    variable argument, 35–36
Mingle, 60
Mixins, 57
Mock objects, 58

N

Name-value pairs, 33
.NET, 115
Nonfunctional requirements
    automated testing of, 11–12
Nonfunctional testing, 186

O

Object-oriented design, 61–71
  abbreviations, 67–68
  class collections and, 70
  dots per line, 66–67
  else keyword, 64–65
  encapsulation of data, 70–71
  entities, 68
  getters/setters properties, 70
  indentation of methods, 63–64
  instance variables, 68–69
  primitives and strings, 65
  rules for, 62
Object-oriented languages, 41
Objects, 21–27
  class methods and chaining, 21–23
  Expression Builder and, 23–26
Orchard, David, 101

P

Pantazopoulos, Stelios, 81
Paradigms, 43–44
Parameters vs. method chaining, 26
Parsons, Rebecca J., 39–49
Performance testing, 185, 197–213
  communication and, 210–211
  defined, 197–198
  meetings and, 200
  process of, 211–213
  requirements gathering, 198–203
  testing, 203–209
  testing vs. production environment,
    205–207
  testing, database size for, 207
Pipeline build, 167, 171f
Playback testing, 10
Polyglot programming, 51–60
  blank parameters, checking for,
    54–55
  future of, 60
  Jaskell and, 55–58
  overview of, 52
  reading files and, 52–54
  testing Java and, 58–60
Polymorphism, 57
Poorly hung methods, 54
Poppendieck, Mary, 75
Poppendieck, Tom, 75
Primitives, 65
Procedural languages, 40

Process, performance testing and,
    211–213
Production environment, 190
Production verification, 187
Production vs. design, 12–13
Programming languages, *see* Computer
    languages
Project tracking tool, 60
Project vital signs, 81
  budget burn-down, 88f, 87–89
  current state of implementation, 89f,
    90f, 89–91
  defined, 81–82
  delivery quality, 86f, 86–87
  vs. information radiators, 82
  vs. project health, 82
  scope burn-up and, 83f, 83–85
  team perceptions and, 91f, 92
Prolog, 42, 48
Properties, moving outside target, 156
Provider contracts, 103–106
  characteristics of, 106

R

Reading files with Groovy, 52–54
Real-time summary, *see* Project vital
    signs
Refactoring, 135–164
  taskname attribute, 159–160
  build files, 136–137
  CI publishers and, 161
  declarations, 143
  defined, 135
  dependencies, 144
  deployment code, 149–150
  descriptions vs. comments, 149
  directories, centralizing, 160
  elements and antlibs, 150–152
  elements, reusing, 154–156
  environment variables, 145
  Exec vs. Apply, 161
  filtersfile, 145–146
  internal targets, 160
  library definitions and filesets,
    152–153
  literal values and properties,
    144–145
  location attribute, 157
  macrodef, 139–141
  move target to wrapper build file,
    147–149

name and description catalog, 137–163

path and option scripts, moving, 157–159

properties files, 146–147

properties, moving outside target, 156

runtime properties, 153–154

target naming, 162–163

targets, extracting, 141–142

when to, 136

Regression testing, 186

Release candidates, 168–169

Reports and metrics, 192

Requirements gathering, 198–203

Robinson, Ian, 93

Royle, Mike, 119

Ruby, 48

anonymous classes (structs) in, 37

duck typing and, 45

evaluation context and, 30

identifiers and, 20

as language, 41

literal hash in, 32

symbols in, 20

Runtime properties, 153–154

S

Scala, 48

Schema versioning, 96–101

Schematron, 102–103

Scheme, 48

Scope burn-up, 83f, 83–85

Security, 165

Sequential context, 19

Sequential languages, 46

Service-level agreements, consumer-driven contracts and, 111

Service-oriented architecture, 93

breaking changes and, 101–103

evolving a service and, 95–96

overview of, 93–94

schema versioning and, 96–101

Set-Based Concurrent Engineering, 78

Simpson, Julian, 135–164

Single-click software release, see Continuous integration

Software

design improvements, 61–62

"Last mile" problem, 5–14

SQL, 42

Staging environment, 189

Static languages, 40

Static typing, 45

Statically typed languages, 41

Strict languages, 46

Strings, 65

Strongly typed, 45

Structs, 37

System integration environment, 188

T

Targets

enforcing names of, 160

extracting, 141–142

naming, 162–163

Team capacity, 77

Teams, perceptions of, 91f, 92

Technical Architecture Group, W3C, 96

Test analysis, 193

Test scripting, 194

Test-driven design (TDD), 12

Test-driven development (TDD), 181

Testing

acceptance tests, 170

automation and, 10

bug counts, 86f, 86–87

commit tests, 168

continuous integration and, 173–174

data validation, 184

database size for, 207

environments, 187–190

exploratory, 183

functional, 182

integration, 183

Java, 58–60

"Last mile" problem and, 11–12

life cycle in waterfall vs. agile projects, 179f, 178–180

nonfunctional, 186

of nonfunctional requirements, 11–12

number of cases needed, 208

in parallel, 12

performance, 185, 203–209

playback, 10

vs. production environment, 205–207

production verification, 187

regression, 186

user acceptance, 184

Third-party interfaces, 207
Thomas, Dave, 38
Threading, 55
Throughput, 198–203
Tools, project, 191
Tuples, 57
Turing completeness, 43
Type characteristics, 44–45
Type interference, 45

U

Unit testing, 181
User acceptance testing, 184

V

Variable argument methods, 35–36
Variables
    context, 19
    in DSL, 20
    environment, 145
    vs. identifiers, 20
    instance, 68–69
Version control systems, 168
Versionless software, 13–14
Vingrys, Kristan, 177

W

W3C Technical Architecture Group on
    versioning strategies, 96
Wall-clock testing, 11
Waterfall vs. Agile test strategy
    data validation, 184
    environments, testing, 187–190
    exploratory testing, 183
    functional testing, 182
    integration testing, 183
    issue management, 190
    nonfunctional testing, 186
    performance testing, 185
    production verification, 187
    regression testing, 186
    reports and metrics for, 192
    test types, 181
    testing roles for, 193f, 193–195
    tools for, 191–192
    unit testing, 181
    user acceptance testing, 184
Waterfall vs. agile test strategy, 177
    testing life cycle, 179f, 178–180
Web service–level agreements, 111
Weirich, Jim, 31, 38

Web 2.0

Welcome to the Web, version 2.0. You need some help to tame the wild technologies out there. Start with *Prototype and script.aculo.us*, a book about two libraries that will make your JavaScript life much easier.

See how to reach the largest possible web audience with *The Accessible Web*.

Prototype and script.aculo.us

Tired of getting swamped in the nitty-gritty of cross-browser, Web 2.0–grade JavaScript? Get back in the game with Prototype and script.aculo.us, two extremely popular JavaScript libraries that make it a walk in the park. Be it Ajax, drag and drop, autocompletion, advanced visual effects, or many other great features, all you need is write one or two lines of script that look so good they could almost pass for Ruby code!

Prototype and script.aculo.us: You never knew JavaScript could do this!
Christophe Porteneuve
(330 pages) ISBN: 1-934356-01-8. $34.95
http://pragprog.com/titles/cppsu

The Accessible Web

The 2000 U.S. Census revealed that 12% of the population is severely disabled. Sometime in the next two decades, one in five Americans will be older than 65. Section 508 of the Americans with Disabilities Act requires your website to provide *equivalent access* to all potential users. But beyond the law, it is both good manners and good business to make your site accessible to everyone. This book shows you how to design sites that excel for all audiences.

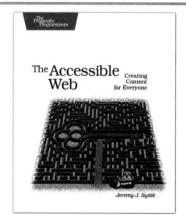

The Accessible Web
Jeremy Sydik
(304 pages) ISBN: 1-934356-02-6. $34.95
http://pragprog.com/titles/jsaccess

Enterprise Ready

Your application is feature complete, but is it ready for the real world? See how to design and deploy production-ready software and *Release It!*.

Did you know Ruby could glue together all sorts of enterprise technologies? See how in *Enterprise Integration with Ruby.*

Release It!

Whether it's in Java, .NET, or Ruby on Rails, getting your application ready to ship is only half the battle. Did you design your system to survive a sudden rush of visitors from Digg or Slashdot? Or an influx of real-world customers from 100 different countries? Are you ready for a world filled with flaky networks, tangled databases, and impatient users?

If you're a developer and don't want to be on call at 3 a.m. for the rest of your life, this book will help.

Design and Deploy Production-Ready Software
Michael T. Nygard
(368 pages) ISBN: 0-9787392-1-3. $34.95
http://pragprog.com/titles/mnee

Enterprise Integration with Ruby

See how to use the power of Ruby to integrate all the applications in your environment. Learn how to
• use relational databases directly and via mapping layers such as ActiveRecord • harness the power of directory services • create, validate, and read XML documents for easy information interchange • use both high- and low-level protocols to knit applications together

Enterprise Integration with Ruby
Maik Schmidt
(360 pages) ISBN: 0-9766940-6-9. $32.95
http://pragprog.com/titles/fr_eir

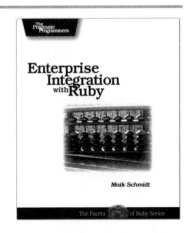

Pragmatic Projects

See what an agile project is supposed to feel like in the award-winning *Practices of an Agile Developer*.

Have you ever noticed that project retrospectives feel too little, too late? What you need to do is start having *Agile Retrospectives*.

Practices of an Agile Developer

Agility is all about using feedback to respond to change. Learn how to apply the principles of agility throughout the software development process
• establish and maintain an agile working environment • deliver what users really want • use personal agile techniques for better coding and debugging • use effective collaborative techniques for better teamwork • move to an agile approach

Practices of an Agile Developer: Working in the Real World
Venkat Subramaniam and Andy Hunt
(189 pages) ISBN: 0-9745140-8-X. $29.95
http://pragprog.com/titles/pad

Agile Retrospectives

Mine the experience of your software development team continually throughout the life of the project. Rather than waiting until the end of the project—as with a traditional retrospective, when it's too late to help—agile retrospectives help you adjust to change *today*.

The tools and recipes in this book will help you uncover and solve hidden (and not-so-hidden) problems with your technology, your methodology, and those difficult "people issues" on your team.

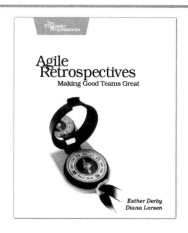

Agile Retrospectives: Making Good Teams Great
Esther Derby and Diana Larsen
(170 pages) ISBN: 0-9776166-4-9. $29.95
http://pragprog.com/titles/dlret

Ruby and Rails

Interested in learning Ruby, or in learning how to use a scripting language the right way? Start with *Everyday Scripting with Ruby: For Teams, Testers, and You.*

If you know Java, and are curious about Ruby on Rails, you don't have to start from scratch. Read *Rails for Java Developers*, and you can catch up to the industry leaders by learning this exciting new technology.

Everyday Scripting with Ruby

Don't waste that computer on your desk. Offload your daily drudgery to where it belongs, and free yourself to do what you should be doing: thinking. All you need is a scripting language (free!), this book (cheap!), and the dedication to work through the examples and exercises. Learn the basics of the Ruby scripting language and see how to create scripts in a steady, controlled way using test-driven design.

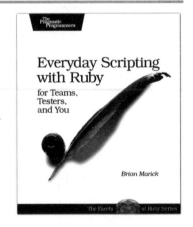

Everyday Scripting with Ruby: For Teams, Testers, and You
Brian Marick
(320 pages) ISBN: 0-9776166-1-4. $29.95
http://pragprog.com/titles/bmsft

Rails for Java Developers

Enterprise Java developers already have most of the skills needed to create Rails applications. They just need a guide which shows how their Java knowledge maps to the Rails world. That's what this book does. It covers: • the Ruby language • building MVC applications • unit and functional testing • security • project automation • configuration • web services This book is the fast track for Java programmers who are learning or evaluating Ruby on Rails.

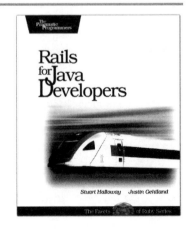

Rails for Java Developers
Stuart Halloway and Justin Gehtland
(300 pages) ISBN: 0-9776166-9-X. $34.95
http://pragprog.com/titles/fr_r4j

Erlang and More

New challenges call for new solutions. The coming multicore crunch makes parallel programming a necessity, not a luxury. Learn how to do it right with *Programming Erlang*.

And whatever language you use, you'll need a good text editor, too. On the Mac, we recommend TextMate.

Programming Erlang

Learn how to write truly concurrent programs—programs that run on dozens or even hundreds of local and remote processors. See how to write high-reliability applications—even in the face of network and hardware failure—using the Erlang programming language.

Programming Erlang: Software for a Concurrent World
Joe Armstrong
(536 pages) ISBN: 1-934356-00-X. $36.95
http://pragprog.com/titles/jaerlang

TextMate

If you're coding Ruby or Rails on a Mac, then you owe it to yourself to get the TextMate editor. And, once you're using TextMate, you owe it to yourself to pick up this book. It's packed with information that will help you automate all your editing tasks, saving you time to concentrate on the important stuff. Use snippets to insert boilerplate code and refactorings to move stuff around. Learn how to write your own extensions to customize it to the way you work.

TextMate: Power Editing for the Mac
James Edward Gray II
(200 pages) ISBN: 0-9787392-3-X. $29.95
http://pragprog.com/titles/textmate

The Pragmatic Bookshelf

The Pragmatic Bookshelf features books written by developers for developers. The titles continue the well-known Pragmatic Programmer style and continue to garner awards and rave reviews. As development gets more and more difficult, the Pragmatic Programmers will be there with more titles and products to help you stay on top of your game.

Visit Us Online

ThoughtWorks Anthology's Home Page
http://pragprog.com/titles/twa
Source code from this book, errata, and other resources. Come give us feedback, too!

Register for Updates
http://pragprog.com/updates
Be notified when updates and new books become available.

Join the Community
http://pragprog.com/community
Read our weblogs, join our online discussions, participate in our mailing list, interact with our wiki, and benefit from the experience of other Pragmatic Programmers.

New and Noteworthy
http://pragprog.com/news
Check out the latest pragmatic developments in the news.

Save on the PDF

Save on the PDF version of this book. Owning the paper version of this book entitles you to purchase the PDF version at a terrific discount. The PDF is great for carrying around on your laptop. It's hyperlinked, has color, and is fully searchable.

Buy it now at pragprog.com/coupon.

Contact Us

Phone Orders:	1-800-699-PROG (+1 919 847 3884)
Online Orders:	www.pragprog.com/catalog
Customer Service:	orders@pragprog.com
Non-English Versions:	translations@pragprog.com
Pragmatic Teaching:	academic@pragprog.com
Author Proposals:	proposals@pragprog.com